# IN THE
# MEANTIME

DONALD
GIBSON

# IN THE
# MEANTIME

### Trusting God While
### Waiting for My Miracle

**ARROWS & STONES**

Unless otherwise noted, all Scripture references are from The New King James Version of the Bible © copyright 1979, 1980, 1982 by Thomas Nelson, Inc., Nashville, Tennessee. | References marked KJV are from the King James Version of the Bible. | References marked ESV are from The Holy Bible, English Standard Version Copyright © 2001 by Crossway Bibles, a division of Good News Publishers. | References marked NLT are from The New Living Translation of the Bible, copyright © 1996 by Tyndale House Publishers, Inc., Wheaton, Illinois. | References marked AMP are from The Amplified Bible, copyright © 1954, 1958, 1962, 1964, 1965, 1987 by The Lockman Foundation, La Habra, California. | 20TH: The Twentieth Century Bible by Robert Addison Dague, Copyright © 1917 by M.E. Cadwallander. | AAT: The Bible, An American Translation, Copyright © 1931 by Edgar J. Goodspeed and J.M. Powis Smith. | ASV: The American Standard Version of the Bible, public domain. | BECK: William Beck's Bible in the Language of Today, also known as The Holy Bible, an American Translation, Copyright © 1963, 1976 by William Beck. | BBE: The Bible in Basic English, (1949) public domain. | BV: The Berkley Version of the Bible, Copyright © 1959 by Zondervan Publishing. | ERB: The Emphasized Bible, Copyright © 1902 by Joseph Bryant Rotherham. | KNOCH: The Concordant Literal Version of the New Testament © 1966 by Adolph Ernst Knoch. | CONDON: The New Testament for the New World, Copyright © 1870 by Kevin Condon. | CONEYBEARE: The Epistles of Paul, Translation of the Epistles of Paul the Apostle by William John Coneybeare, public domain. | CPG: The Cotton Patch Version of the New Testament © 1968–1972, by Clarence Jordan. | FENTON: The Holy Bible in Modern English translated by Ferrar Fenton (1903), public domain. | GODBEY: Translation of the New Testament from the Original Greek by Rev. W.B. Godbey (1902), public domain. | GNB: The Good News Translation of the Bible, Copyright © 1976, 1992 by American Bible Society. | LAUBACH: The Inspired Letters In Clearest English prepared by Frank C. Laubach (1956), public domain. | MNT: A New Translation of the Bible, Copyright © 1926, 1954, 1964 by James Moffatt. | NASB: The New American Standard Bible, Copyright © 1960, 1962, 1963, 1968, 1971, 1972, 1973, 1975, 1977 by the Lockman Foundation. | NBV: The Modern Language Bible, the New Berkeley Version in Modern English, Copyright © 1969 by Zondervan Publishing House. | NEB: The New English Bible, Copyright © by Oxford University Press and Cambridge University Press 1961, 1971. | NLV: The New Life Version of the Bible Copyright © 1969 by Christian Literature Internationa. | NIV: The New International Version of the Bible, Copyright © 1973, 1978, 1984 by International Bible Society. | NORLIE: Norlie's Simplified New Testament In Plain English–For Today's Reader. A New Translation from the Greek by Olaf Morgan Norlie, Copyright © 1961 by Zondervan Publishing. | PME: The Phillips New Testament in Modern English © 1958 by J.B. Phillips. | PEB: The Plain English Bible, Copyright © 1952 by Charles K. Williams. | RIEU: The Gospel of Matthew, Copyright © 1957 by C.H. Rieu. | RSV: The Revised Standard Version of the Bible, Copyright © 1946, 1952, 1971, 1973 by the Division of Christian Education of the National Council of the Churches of Christ in the U.S.A. | TLB: The Living Bible paraphrased by Kenneth Taylor, Copyright © 1971 by Tyndale House Publishers. | TRANSLATORS: The Translator's New Testament, Copyright © 2005 by Alvin Cordes. | WADE: The Documents of the New Testament, Copyright © 1934 by

G. W. Wade. | WAND: The New Testament Letters Prefaced and Paraphrased by J. W. C. Wand, Copyright © 1944, 1650 by J.W.C. Wand. | WAY: The Letters of St. Paul to seven churches and three friends with the Letter to the Hebrews Translated by Arthur S. Way (1901), public domain. | WEYMOUTH: The New Testament in Modern Speech by Richard Francis Weymouth © 2002, Christian Classics Ethereal Library. | WORRELL: The New Testament Revised and Translated by A. S. Worrell (1904), public domain. | WUEST: Wuest's Expanded Translation of the Greek New Testament, Copyright © 1959 by Kenneth S. Wuest. | YLT: Young's Literal Translation of the Holy Bible by Robert Young (1862), public domain

For foreign and subsidiary rights, contact the author.

Cover design by: Sara Young

Cover photo by: Ryan Holzaepfel

ISBN: 978-1-957369-45-7     1 2 3 4 5 6 7 8 9 10

Printed in the United States of America

*A special thank you to Beth Bowles for your involvement in this process. You have a unique gift to capture a project and make it shine! The work we have done together all these years, I will forever be indebted to you for. Thank you for building the kingdom of God with us.*

*To my Pastors Larry and Sharon Jones. Thank you for giving me an opportunity in ministry when I was at my sickest. You have both been so instrumental in my life and my journey. The only way I know to pay back your investment is to pay it forward in the lives of so many others.*

*To my amazing wife, Jonna. You truly have wowed me over the years and the courage to walk this journey with me has been breathtaking at times. I will never have enough words to express my love to you and appreciation for you. To my boys, there is greatness in you. I pray you live your lives in the realm of miracles and the grace of God. You are the greatest treasure in your me and your mom's life.*

*To my mom and dad, Brenda and Donald Gibson Sr. You have loved me unconditionally and have challenged me to be a better son, father, and husband. I love you more than you will ever know.*

*To Mercy Gate Church, our staff, board, and to Freeport First, the two churches I have had the privilege of leading. Thank you for going on the journey with me to see the genuineness of Jesus as well as the miraculous. Thank you for the latitude to grow and chase after the heartbeat of God.*

*To the reader, I pray that my healing journey will stir your faith, infuse you with hope, and encourage you to believe for the miraculous in your life. As God has healed me completely, I know that He will do it again and even greater for you!*

# CONTENTS

NOW MAY THE GOD OF HOPE
FILL YOU WITH ALL JOY AND
PEACE IN BELIEVING, THAT YOU
MAY ABOUND IN HOPE BY THE
POWER OF THE HOLY SPIRIT.

ROMANS 15:13

# INTRODUCTION

heard it said once that "Principles are taught, but miracles must be caught." Miracles have a unique way of accelerating the principles. I wonder if that is the reason David wrote, *"For a day in your courts is better than a thousand elsewhere"* (Psalm 84:10, ESV). Could David have known that a day in the presence of the Lord would accelerate his process and the principles the Lord was teaching him through that process?

To realize you are in the presence of an awesome and amazing God is truly a miracle in itself, and in that atmosphere, the principles that have been poured into our lives can be expedited in a moment. This is more than being in church; it's about being in His presence, acknowledging that very fact, then expecting a miraculous God to do something in your life, the miracle you need at that very moment. This confident expectancy in the Lord is called *hope*.

The story of the five loaves and two fish has intrigued me for years … a happy meal, if you please. The Bible records it this way:

> *Then He commanded the multitudes to sit down on the grass. And He took the five loaves and the two fish, and looking up to heaven, He blessed and broke and gave the loaves to the disciples; and the disciples gave to the multitudes. So they all ate and were filled, and they took up twelve baskets full of the fragments that remained. Now those who had eaten were about five thousand men, besides women and children.*
> Matthew 14:19–21

The Scriptures say Jesus took it, blessed it, broke it, and gave it to the disciples; then, they gathered the leftovers. My whole life I had read this story, and I'd even preached it a time or two. Then one day it dawned on me: Jesus did so much more than feed five thousand people that day. He did much more than just break bread with them.

Jesus, first of all, *is* the Bread of Life (see John 6:35 and 48). So the Bread of Life knew something about bread, but more importantly, He knew something about bread that sustains. He didn't just break those five loaves and two fish; He broke the limitations that were on those five loaves and two fish, and they then did what they could not do before.

In the natural, that lunch was limited to feeding just one boy, but when Jesus broke the limitations off of it, it suddenly had the capacity to feed multitudes. So much so that when the meal was over, all said and done, the leftovers (twelve basketfuls) were more than the original.

Wow! Could it be that if today, in the twenty-first century, we placed our lives in the hands of the Master and prayed something like: "Lord Jesus, take me, bless me and break me," that He would break the limitations off of our lives too, no matter what those limitations seemed to be? The answer, of course, is a resounding **YES**!

Limitations and needed miracles are different for each person. To a single mom, the miracle she needs may be a day of rest or even just someone showing her kindness. To a father, his needed miracle could be feeling appreciation from his wife and children for what he does on a daily basis to sustain the family. For the woman in the Bible who had suffered with *"an issue of blood"* for twelve years, her needed miracle was getting through the crowds to touch Jesus and be healed (see Matthew 9:190–22, KJV). To the person who is dying of some disease, the miracle could come in a couple of manners: (1) The Lord could heal them and remove their sickness, or (2) The Lord could call them Home. Either way, for the believer, we win.

This is the story of my miracle. Beginning when I was seventeen and continuing for the next twelve years, I suffered from Crohn's disease. I could not live a normal life, was often hospitalized and had to undergo surgery to remove parts of my intestines affected by the disease. I was finally told by a specialist that I had the worst case of Crohn's disease he had ever seen and would have to submit to additional surgery to remove the rest of my intestines and then be fitted with a colostomy bag. And, he said, I needed to do this quickly if my life was to be spared.

But God had another plan. He took me through a process that taught me the true meaning of hope, and then, in my darkest hour, He healed me instantly and completely. I pray as you read this book documenting my journey that the Lord Jesus will break the limitations off of your life and that the biblical principles you have come to know, read about or heard about are accelerated because of the miraculous in your life.

Donald Gibson
Texas

# PROLOGUE

ngulfed in heat, everywhere I walked in our home was hot! The heat was so intense that I didn't know whether to ask God to stop it or to allow it to continue. As consumed as I was with this phenomenon (I felt as if I was burning up), externally, I was cool to the touch. What was going on?

The presence and the glory of the Lord had filled my home. It was emotionally overwhelming, but at the same time, I was feeling better physically than I had since I was a teenager. Could this be the answer to all my prayers, all my tears, all my questionings? Could God really be coming through for me at last? I, for one, was sure of it. And medical tests would soon prove me right. My miracle had come, but not before I had taken a journey and come to understand the process of hope.

Let me start from the beginning of my journey so that you can understand where I am coming from. A miracle can better be fully appreciated when it is clear where a person has come from and what he has come through to get to that point of excitement and victory in his life. This, then, is my story.

> *"Crohn's disease is an inflammatory disease of the intestines that may affect any part of the gastrointestinal tract, causing a wide variety of symptoms. It primarily causes abdominal pain, diarrhea, vomiting or weight loss, but may also cause complications outside of the gastrointestinal tract such as skin rashes, arthritis and inflammation of the eyes. Being an auto-immune disease in which the body's immune system attacks the gastrointestinal tract causing inflammation, it is classified as a type of inflammatory bowel disease. There is no known pharmaceutical or surgical cure for Crohn's disease. Treatment options are restricted to controlling symptoms, maintaining remission, and preventing relapse."[1]*
>
> Wikipedia, the online Encyclopedia

---

1  "Crohn's Disease," Wikipedia (Wikimedia Foundation), https://en.wikipedia.org/wiki/Crohn%27s_disease.

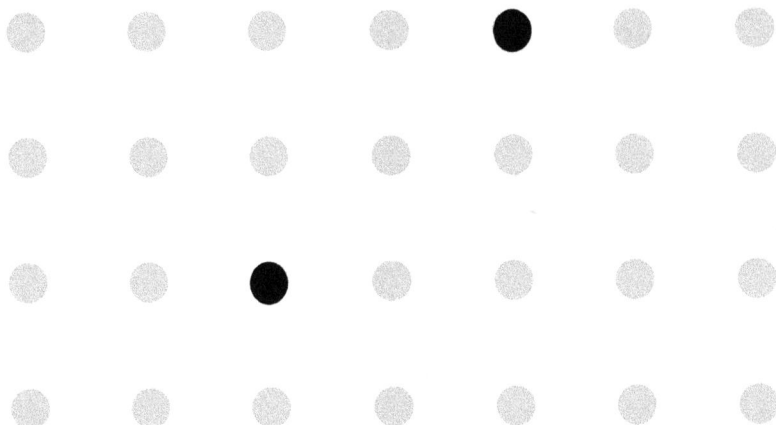

# A LETTER FROM ORAL ROBERTS

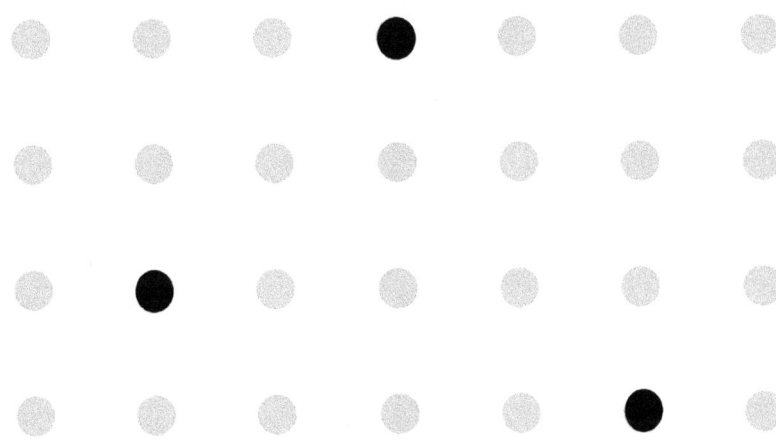

Dear Donald,

We have received your letter in which you shared your miracle healing testimony of how God, through a Word of Knowledge I spoke when I was a guest on the Praise the Lord program about 12 years ago, healed you. He is truly a good God and I praise Him along with you for how He healed and sustained you throughout these years.

Donald, I'm glad you let me know about your miracle healing from the profound afflictions of Crohn's disease. And I'm believing for the power of God's Spirit to continue moving *in* and *through* your life with MIRACLES!

It is always a blessing to me to receive testimonies from those who have received a healing touch from God through this ministry. It seems that lately, I am hearing from many like yourself, who were healed many years ago but are just now letting me know about it.

Hebrews 4:12 says, "The word that God speaks is alive and full of power, active, energizing, effective, and sharper than any two-edged sword." Matthew 24:35 also declares, "Heaven and earth shall pass away, but My Word shall not pass away." If we build our lives on the Word of God, the Bible says that we will be like the man who built his house upon the rock. When the storms began to rage, his house stood strong (Matthew 7:24). Praise God, that tells me that we can stake our lives on the Word!

Donald, I am 89 years old now and in the sunset of this life, but I am committed to finishing my course. I send to you a blessing of the "Old Prophet," for the further enrichment of your life in Christ and the success of all you undertake in His Name.

Thank you again for taking the time to share your testimony of healing with me. I fully expect to see you in Heaven.

Sincerely,

Oral Roberts

P.S. I hope you receive this; your letter was returned when we used the address on your letterhead.

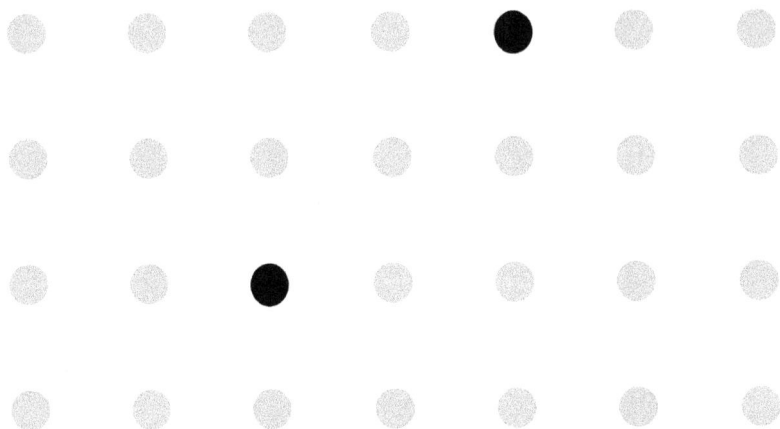

# CHAPTER 1

# A ROAD TO PROMISE

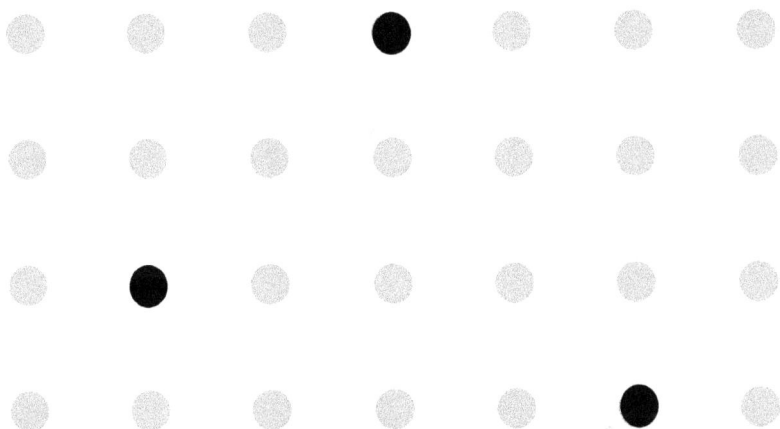

was born blue, with my umbilical cord wrapped around my neck three times. I don't know whether I was just excited to get into this world or the devil was attempting to take me out before I ever got here. One thing is sure: it frightened my parents and their doctors. Mom tells me that the doctors had to work to revive me because the cord around my neck was cutting off my breath.

After we were home for three days, I once again turned blue, and Mom rushed me to the emergency room and issued a strong warning to the doctors: "I don't want him back until he is fixed." Thank goodness her response was quick; without it, I might not be here today. Apparently, I was "fixed," at least for the moment.

My primary years were very typical for a kid raised in the great state of Texas. I enjoyed what other little boys enjoyed: making mud pies, hunting for frogs, spiders and other insects and leaving little surprises for my mom to find while doing the laundry.

When I was five, we moved to a little Texas town called Sweeny, the home of the Fighting Bulldogs. I attended school there while learning to play baseball and tennis.

Sweeny was an incredible place to grow up. There was just one stoplight (plus one blinking caution light) in the entire town. Today that little town remains important to me for a couple of reasons: (1) My parents still live there, and (2) It was in Sweeny that I was introduced to the Gospel. There, some good people taught me (or attempted to teach me) the Word of God.

I wasn't the easiest child to teach. As a boy, I believe I must have had ADD (Attention Deficit Disorder) before there were words to describe it. Back then, it was just thought of as being a busy, energetic little boy. The neat thing was that if I did have ADD, then so did all of my friends.

One particular Sunday morning, when I was just seven years old, our children's pastor shared with us a story entitled "Teddy's Little House," complete with flannel-board cutouts. As the story went, Teddy lived in a rundown, dilapidated, little house with a broken picket fence and shattered windows. One day a man, who happened to be a carpenter, came by and saw the shabby little house and asked Teddy if he would like to have it repaired and made like brand new again. The carpenter offered to move in and go to work immediately to repair and make new all the broken things. If his offer was accepted, he would also clean the house entirely inside and outside and make it a wonderful place for Teddy to live.

Teddy was very excited about all of this, and so he replied that the carpenter was welcome to move in and fix everything that needed to be repaired and also to do the necessary cleaning.

At that point in the story, the pastor placed a different picture of Teddy's little house on the flannel-board. In this picture, everything had been repaired: the fence was fixed, the windows were new and clean, and Teddy was standing on the front porch with the carpenter who had done all the wonderful work. The carpenter spoke and said, "Teddy, welcome home!"

Our children's pastor then told us that this carpenter's name was Jesus, and Teddy's little house was actually his heart, the place where Jesus is supposed to live. Because Teddy invited the Carpenter (Jesus) into his house (his life), Jesus cleaned up that house and gave both Teddy and Himself a good place to live together.

The pastor then asked us the same question that had been asked of Teddy: "Who here today would like to have that same Carpenter move into your life and clean it up and repair all the broken places?" I immediately threw my hand into the air, and I gave my life to Jesus that very day. For the first time, at seven years of age, I had come to realize that I needed Jesus to move into my life and clean me up because my house was surely dirty.

Today, thirty-eight years later, that story is as real to me as it was the first time I heard it. That was the day God placed me in hope. I was captivated by a divine expectation from Him.

The Bible says, *"May the God of hope fill you with all joy and peace in believing, that you may abound in hope by the power of the Holy Spirit"* (Romans 15:13). The same verse in the Amplified Bible begins, *"May the God of your hope . . . ."* He is a God of hope, and He is the God of my hope (and yours).

Hope is more than anticipation, more than an expected end; it is confident expectancy. This word *hope* stands for both the act of hoping (see Romans 4:18 and 1 Corinthians 9:10) and the thing hoped for (see Colossians 1:5 and 1 Peter 1:3).

. . . . . . . . . . . . . . . . . . . . . . . . . . . . . . . .

## Hope is more than anticipation, more than an expected end; it is confident expectancy.

. . . . . . . . . . . . . . . . . . . . . . . . . . . . . . . .

In the Christian experience, hope is part of our foundation. This word *hope* is found in the Bible 129 times, and most of the time it means to be in expectation or to wait patiently on something from the Lord.

When I invited Jesus to live in my house, I became a prisoner of hope. The Scriptures say, *"As for you also, because of your covenant, I will set your prisoners free from the waterless pit. Return to the stronghold, you prisoners of hope. Even today I declare that I will restore double to you"* (Zechariah 9:11–13). This does not require that we be perfect. If we fail, if we sin, we have an advocate with the Father (see 1 John 2:1). We are not bound or chained to our mistakes or to our dirty, broken things. We can be free from the guilt of yesterday, all because we have hope in our God of hope. Oh, I am so glad to be a prisoner of hope!

Hope is an emotional mechanism within us, and I believe that our passion for the things of God derives from that hope. Even at seven, I was excited about my new relationship with Jesus, and my passion was obvious to everyone. I went straight home from church that day and began reading the Bible (in the book of Genesis, because I didn't know where else to begin). I had to ask my mother the meaning of every other word, but I was thrilled because I knew I was saved and Jesus had moved into my heart, and my life now belonged to Him.

From that time forward, I got involved in everything I possibly could at church. You name it, and I wanted to be a part of it. My mother was over the ministry of ladies, so I would go to ladies' functions with her. And that's the place to go to learn how to pray! Those women knew how to touch God, and they impacted me at the same time they were praying for other things and other people.

At first, when I heard how these godly women prayed, I didn't know whether to be excited or scared. One thing was certain: I hungered for what they had. Don't get me wrong; I was still all boy and continued to get into plenty of trouble, but now most of it was at church.

When I reached eleven years of age, I went to kid's camp and experienced another dramatic change in my life. On the third night of the camp, the speaker addressed the subject of the "Baptism in the Holy Spirit." I was somewhat familiar with what he was saying because I had been raised in a charismatic church where the spiritual gifts were used quite regularly in the services, and so I had often heard people speak in tongues. Still, I thought this was just for adults, especially the church leadership, and of course, the pastor was the main guy to have it. I really hadn't understood that an eleven-year-old kid could be filled with the Holy Spirit.

I knew the Holy Spirit had moved into me when I was saved, but the camp speaker was preaching that instead of the Holy Spirit just being in me, I could be in Him. He demonstrated this to us by using a water-filled pitcher (representing the Holy Spirit) and a cup (representing us). When a person asked Jesus into his heart, the pitcher poured the Holy Spirit into his life until the cup was completely full to running over. I could relate to that because that was exactly what I had felt like when I got saved.

But then the speaker took the cup and plunged it into the pitcher of water and said, "This is what it is to be filled with the Holy Spirit." I didn't understand all the theology of what he was saying, but I knew I wanted to be placed in that "Pitcher." So I responded to the altar call, and it was almost unbelievable what happened to me next and throughout the next day and a half.

I began speaking in a language I had never learned or even heard. From that moment, I literally could not function normally. I prayed, cried and spoke in a foreign language until two o'clock the next morning.

The camp counselors eventually took me to my room and placed me on a bottom bunk—not the top bunk I had been using until then (because they were afraid I would fall off).

The next day the phenomenon continued; I could not speak English the entire day. When asked by a friend if I wanted to play softball and what position I wanted to play, my response, which I intended to be "second base," came out in that foreign language, so I just didn't play.

I imagine that most eleven-year-olds would have been frightened or intimidated to have such a thing happen to them, but I felt an awesome peace, and I knew Jesus was close by and that it was He who had placed me in the Pitcher (the Holy Ghost). I'm not trying to present some form of theological understanding here. I'm just telling it the way it happened to me.

I think we try to keep God within our formulas too often, and then we get frustrated with Him when our formulas don't work because He chooses to do something different.

This reminds me of the time when I was seven, and I asked my dad for a shotgun for Christmas. Mom said, "There ain't no way you're gettin' a shotgun at seven years old."

But I pulled Dad aside and said to him, "Come on, Dad! Don't listen to her," and I was so sure he would do it that I got my hopes up.

Christmas morning came, and I opened up every one of the presents with my name on it, and I didn't get a shotgun. Boy, was I disappointed! I got some nice things, but it wasn't what I wanted. I subconsciously rejected each of those other things because it was not my expected desire.

Many of us have had this experience spiritually. God blesses us on every side, but we have an expected desire (a hope), and what we are receiving doesn't measure up to it. We're hoping for something greater.

The enemy tries to tell us that we shouldn't have that hope and that we will never receive our promise. Many times hope *does* seem to be deferred, and we think God has forgotten or abandoned us because He hasn't done things our way or in our desired timing. In those moments, we need to take a careful look at all the little gifts around because they will lead us to the next place in our journey. We must keep trusting God until He gives us the desired expectancy.

. . . . . . . . . . . . . . . . . . . . . . . . . . . . .

## The enemy tries to tell us that we shouldn't have that hope and that we will never receive our promise.

. . . . . . . . . . . . . . . . . . . . . . . . . . . . .

Paul declared to the Corinthians, *"If in this life only we have hope in Christ, we are of all men the most pitiable"* (1 Corinthians 15:19). We can't hope only in this world, and we can't hope only in the things of this world. We must hope in God. This is the hope that eventually brings results.

That Christmas morning, the last package Momma gave me was pajamas. I ripped the paper off it, and when I saw what it was, man, was I depressed! I tried to hide it and said, "Ah . . . thank you," and I hugged my parents.

Dad asked me, "Junior, did you get everything you wanted?"

I lied conveniently, "Yes, sir."

He said, "Really? Well there's one more little gift under the tree. It's a little box, and I think it has your name on it."

I went back to the tree, rummaged around until I found that gift and then quickly opened it. Inside the box was nothing but a piece of paper. It was a riddle directing me to go to the mailbox. With renewed hope, I took off down to the end of the road. Grabbing open the mailbox, I found another little box inside.

My hope was rising, being renewed, and I thought to myself, "I AM getting a shotgun." But each little box led to the next, and over the coming minutes, I ran all over those five acres.

One of the riddles took me to a deer stand on the back of the property, and there was another box. Now, with each box, although it was encouraging that I was on the right trail, hope was being deferred, and that was hard for a seven-year-old.

Finally, after seven or eight boxes and what seemed to me to be an eternity, the last riddle sent me to Dad's truck. I crawled all over the bed of that truck, but found nothing. I looked under the truck, and there was nothing. Finally, I opened the cab of the truck, and there in Dad's gun rack was a .410 shotgun with a Christmas bow tied to it. How happy I was! That was a GREAT Christmas!

I had initially been discouraged because the package didn't come the way I expected it, but ultimately I received the expected result because I didn't give up hope. This is a lesson all of us must learn.

When we accept Jesus, He places us in hope, and He begins a process in us. But then, no matter how God chooses to work in you, be assured that you serve a God of hope, and if you are faithful and don't lose hope, you will receive the expected end. He guarantees it.

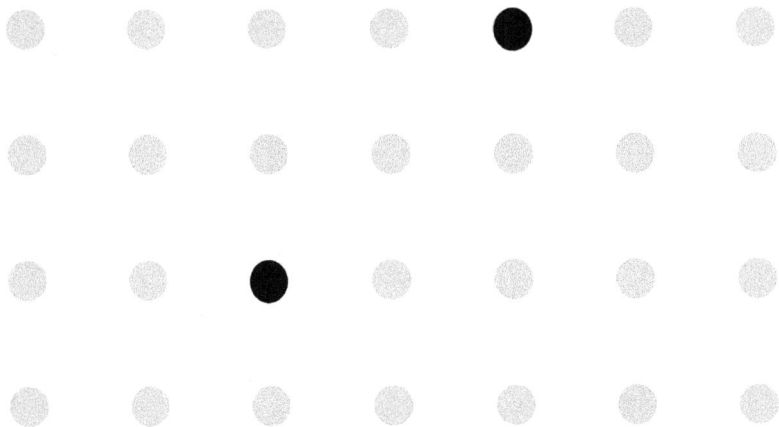

# CHAPTER 2

# THE PROCESS

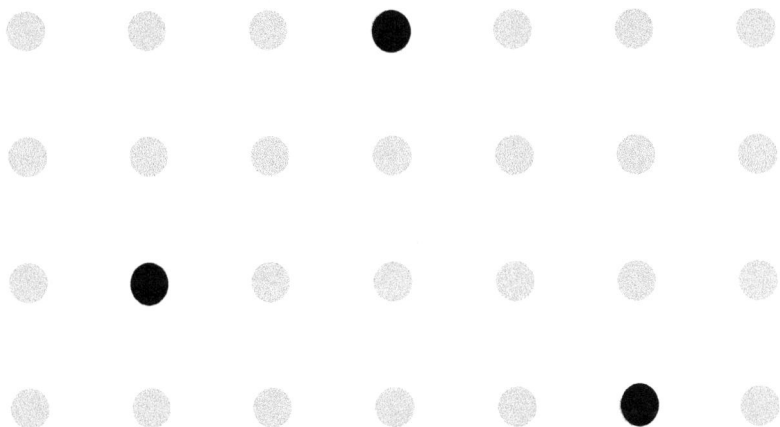

After my experience at kid's camp, I made some serious promises to the Lord. I felt like Peter in the Bible when he told Jesus, "All those others may forsake You and run out on You, Jesus, but I never will." Jesus looked at Peter, with all the love in His heart, and told His erring disciple, "Before the sun comes up and the rooster crows, you will deny Me three times" (see Matthew 26:34). The sad truth is that the third time Peter was challenged, he actually cursed the very name of Jesus.

I have to say that was me! In the eighth grade, I made a serious proclamation of all the things I would do for the Lord and all the things I certainly would *not* do in the world, but before my freshman year in high school, I had already broken every promise. Where had my all spiritual passion gone?

This word *passion* can be defined as "an intense, driving, or over-mastering feeling or conviction." It is a strong desire that propels us into action. It can also be likened to a hunger or thirst, an appetite that craves to be satisfied. True passion comes through our hope and a connection with God through the Lord Jesus. When I accepted Jesus, I immediately had an intense passion and was called to action. But, although I still had that connection, my passion had waned over time.

There are many things that can quench spiritual passion. Among them are the following: the desire for acceptance and approval from people, passivity, apathy, lack of purpose, and allowing the precious to become common and familiar. In our society today, tolerance, political correctness, bipartisanship, and compromise are keywords that can and often do lead to a decline in our passion for the Lord.

Passion is like a magnet. It will either draw people to you or push them away. If we are not strong and healthy in our convictions, we are concerned more about what others think than about our promises to and from God.

Truly passionate people don't care what others think. They will die for their principles and values. But when passion wanes, hope suffers, and the connection with God is weakened. Too often, that is when we begin to look for substitutes.

. . . . . . . . . . . . . . . . . . . . . . . . . . . . . . . .

## Truly passionate people don't care what others think. They will die for their principles and values.

. . . . . . . . . . . . . . . . . . . . . . . . . . . . . . . .

Different people find substitutes in different places. Some turn to sex, some to drugs, and some to other forms of entertainment. We live in a sex-crazed culture and society that thrives on entertainment. If you Google the word *passion*, you will find two strong and yet totally different definitions: (1) The Gospel truth of Jesus' death, and (2) Sexually driven things of this world. One of these is clearly a counterfeit, and the other is real. The fact is that people are seeking a passionate reason for living. The awesome truth is this: Jesus doesn't give up on us as quickly as others, not even as quickly as we give up on ourselves.

Now I was out doing my own thing. There were some things I could not bring myself to do because I still had a sense of the presence of the Lord being right there with me, but this compromised way of living continued until I was seventeen.

Please understand me here. I didn't just jump into sin overnight; it happened over a period of time. Sometimes I was a sinner, and sometimes I was a saint. Through it all, I remained faithful to church and could even play the "religious game." I was there for every service and knew when to sing, when to pray, and when to raise my hands. But in reality, I wasn't fooling anyone, especially not myself or God.

During this time, I even learned the art of making myself cry to look repentant, but there was no change in my behavior. I was sorry, but not repentant. Some might say that I had lost my salvation, but I'm not so sure of that. I could still feel the sting of the Holy Spirit in my heart, and again, there were some things I still would not or could not do.

Have you ever noticed that the enemy tempts us with the very same things he tempted Jesus with? There, on the mount of temptation, he said to Christ: "If you are ... command these stones to become bread. If you are ... bow down to me. If you are ... cast yourself off the pinnacle" (see Matthew 4 and Luke 4), and he does the same thing to us today. He says, "If you truly loved God so much, you wouldn't be going through this. If you really heard from God, you wouldn't be in this trouble. If God was really for you and not against you, you wouldn't be facing this thing."

As a result of this, when things are not working out right, you might be tempted to ask God, "Where are You?" Maybe your children haven't come back to the Lord like you thought they would, or maybe you have been sick in your body. You are believing for a miracle, but instead of receiving a miracle, things seem to be getting worse. You have a dream and a vision, but it seems that, for some unknown reason, they have been delayed.

When this happens, it's tempting to say to the person who is suffering so, "You must have lost your faith." It might be more accurate to say that such a person has "lost hope." Faith comes by education, but hope is an emotion. *"Faith comes by hearing and hearing by the word of God"* (Romans 10:17), but hope is an emotional mechanism that God has implanted within us. It is an anticipated expectation of what He will do.

God is an emotional God, and He created you and me in His likeness. He gets angry, and He gets happy. Psalm 2 shows us that God will actually laugh at His enemies:

*He who sits in the heavens shall laugh;*
*The Lord shall hold them in derision.*
Psalm 2:4

When God is in you, your enemies become God's enemies, so then God laughs at your enemies. This means that when your enemy is coming against you, there ought to be times when you have a belly-flopping laugh because you were created in the image and likeness of your God, and your God is laughing at the enemies who are threatening you.

God knows there is no way your enemy or your circumstance can triumph over you, and so the key is for you to maintain hope through the process and through your circumstances, whatever they may be.

God has a way of using life and life experiences to get our attention. I don't know if He actually *causes* the circumstances that make us fail. As a matter of fact, I'm sure He doesn't, because the Bible says: *"Let no one say, when he is tempted, 'I am tempted by God,' for God cannot be tempted by evil, nor does He Himself tempt anyone. But each one is tempted when he is drawn away by his own desires and enticed. Then, when desire has conceived, it gives birth to sin; and sin, when it is full-grown, brings forth death"* (James 1:13–15). God doesn't cause it, but He also won't waste a good opportunity to get our attention.

. . . . . . . . . . . . . . . . . . . . . . . . . . . . . . . . . . .

# God has a way of using life and life experiences to get our attention.

. . . . . . . . . . . . . . . . . . . . . . . . . . . . . . . . . . .

The Bible also says, in Romans 8:28, *"We know that all things work together for good to those who love God. . . ."* It does not say these things *are* good. Rather, it indicates that they will be *for* our good. Too many times, we think everything should be good about the process, but that is exactly what it is—a process, a process that each person must go through individually with the Lord Jesus Christ. We have hope and confidence that it will all be for our good, but during the process, it is sometimes difficult to find the good in what we are experiencing.

Consider the much-heralded life of Joseph, as recorded in the book of Genesis. From Genesis chapters 37 through chapter 45, we can read about what I have come to call "The Process of Joseph's Life." To the natural eye, things looked bleak for this young man. It appeared that God had forgotten this "dreamer," but even when we feel as if God has forgotten us, He still has a plan. I suppose our struggle comes because we can't presently see or understand the purpose of the process. God, however, has understood it all along. He said through the prophet Isaiah: *"For My thoughts are not your thoughts, nor are your ways My ways"* (Isaiah 55:8). That's why we must learn to trust Him.

Joseph was about seventeen when he had a dream of one day being in a great position of leadership. Then, however, he went through a thirteen-year process before he could come into the fulfillment of that dream. And the road to the realization of his dream was a painful and unwanted one for Joseph.

Think about it. This young man knew where God wanted him to go, and he thought he was in the place where God wanted him to be. And yet, because he tried in his own wisdom and in his own timing to declare his position, he was hated by his brothers and thrown into a pit and left for dead. (It often seems that the ones who should love you the most are the ones who can hurt you the most.)

But Joseph did not allow bitterness to get into his spirit, and when the opportunity came for him to repay his brothers, he did so with kindness rather than doing them harm. I think the process had a lot to do with that. Let me explain.

The processes of life that we go through have the potential to expose our attitudes, as well as shape our attitudes. We can choose to allow these processes to make us bitter or better. Joseph chose to become the man his father Jacob knew he could be and the man God was molding him to become.

· · · · · · · · · · · · · · · · · · · · · · · · · · · · · · · · · · · · ·

# The processes of life that we go through have the potential to expose our attitudes, as well as shape our attitudes.

· · · · · · · · · · · · · · · · · · · · · · · · · · · · · · · · · · · · ·

We all get this opportunity to choose whether the difficult times of life will make us into the person God is shaping us to be or whether we will rebel against the process, allowing bitterness, unforgiveness and the pain of our past to define us.

I once heard it said that storms build character, but I beg to differ. Instead, I believe storms *reveal* character. Storms have a way of exposing what is already in the heart of a person.

Don't get me wrong; we each still have the choice of how we respond to the storm, but what is in a person's character is what comes out in troubled times. The process Joseph went through revealed what was in his heart.

Eventually, Joseph was sold into slavery, but even in that horrible state, he faithfully served a man by the name of Potiphar ... until Potiphar's wife got her eye on him. How would Joseph respond now?

There is something that too often happens in us when we know we have a promise and are anointed for a position, we know God has given a revelatory word for our life, family, job, or business, but that word doesn't seem to be lining up with reality. Sometimes, in this way, your dreams can frustrate you, and your promises can actually begin to aggravate you.

So how do you respond when you are doing the right thing, but the wrong results seem to come? You're trying to live a life of trust and faith, but it seems that things are getting worse and not better. Do you get angry and bitter with God? Or do you realize that you are in a process moving toward a greater purpose?

The truth is the devil isn't after your dream; he is after your hope. He is trying to cause you to give up on God, trying to convince you that God has forgotten you and that God's Word won't work in your life. But always remember that the devil is a liar. God's Word will work IF WE KEEP OUR HOPE.

Faith is about miracles; hope is about morale. It is also about momentum. The devil will not fight you on the basis of faith because you have too much Word in you for him to ever win that fight. Instead, he will fight against your hope. Because God made us emotional creatures, we sometimes get on an emotional roller coaster. We believe God on Monday, but, like those who taunted David in Psalm 42, by Thursday we are asking, "God, where are you?" (see Psalm 42:3). In Psalm 39, David sang: *"My hope is in You. . . ."* (Psalm 39:7). The source of our hope must always be God alone.

Hebrews 11:1 states, *"Faith is the substance of things hoped for, the evidence of things not seen."* Faith, hope and love go hand-in-hand. They are like three cords braided together. If you untwist them and leave them standing alone, just one of them can be weak. The reason the enemy will always attack you first in the element of hope is that he wants to diminish your hope. Then he can go after your faith.

The Bible says that we are not ignorant of the enemy's devices (see 2 Corinthians 2:11). So be diligent in guarding your hope.

Joseph was doing the right thing, but Potiphar's wife, angry with him because he refused her sexual advances, told a lie about him. She claimed that Joseph had tried to forcibly violate her, so Potiphar had Joseph thrown into prison. Once again, Joseph had done the right thing and gotten the wrong results.

But the prison was just another step toward the palace, and it had been part of *the* plan all along. It would not have been the kind of road Joseph wanted to travel or willingly chose. None of us want that. We somehow believe that it should be the will of God for our road to be easy and painless. It rarely is.

I look at this new turn of events in Joseph's life as a test of his motives, and ours need to be tested as well. Why do we do what we do? Is it just for a certain desired result or is it because we want to please our Lord, and we're willing to leave the results to Him? *That* is what I call faith!

For those who are unfamiliar with the ending of Joseph's amazing story, even after having been wrongfully imprisoned in that hated prison, he once again found incredible favor with those in authority. God has you on a road to promise, and you will find favor in the most unfavorable of circumstances.

One day, while still in prison, Joseph had a conversation with two of the king's servants who had also been imprisoned because they had displeased the Pharaoh. One of them had been his chief baker, and the other his chief butler. There, in prison, both men had dreamed dreams in the same night and were looking for someone to interpret them. Joseph had a reputation around the place as a man who could interpret dreams. This was his gift.

Proverbs 18:16 declares, *"A man's gift makes room for him and brings him before great men."* This is what happened to Joseph and his gift of interpreting dreams. Your gift may not seem significant to you, but in the right environment and under the right circumstances, that gift can make a way for you.

Joseph interpreted the two strange dreams. He told the baker that in three days, he would be sentenced to death and would be hanged, and he told the butler that in the same period of time, he would be restored to his former position of service in Pharaoh's house. The two men were grateful to Joseph, and he asked the butler to remember him to Pharaoh after being restored to service and to tell his master of this unjust imprisonment.

The dreams soon came true, just as Joseph had interpreted them. The baker was sentenced to death and hanged, while the butler was restored to his position in the house of Pharaoh. This speaks to us today of the biblical fact: "*the letter killeth but the spirit giveth life*" (2 Corinthians 3:6, KJV).

As most people would, in the excitement of his good fortune the butler forgot Joseph, and for the next two years did not think about his petition. But God was in control, and after this time had passed, the Pharaoh himself had a dream that required interpretation, and this caused the butler to remember Joseph. And, because Joseph was able to interpret the Pharaoh's dream, he was promoted from prison to the palace in a single day. My point is this: even though you are in the process, and everyone else seems to have forgotten you, God *has* not, and He *will* not. He knows exactly where you are, and He has a specific timeline for you and the dreams He has implanted within your spirit.

Bear in mind that God always has the bigger picture in mind, other than simply blessing you. He promoted Joseph so that he would be in a position to take care of his father and his brothers in the future. And God has a great purpose for your life and mine, even though we often don't understand the process. Nevertheless, we can confidently believe the promise of the Scriptures: "*And we know that all things work together for good to those who love God, to those who are the called according to His purpose*" (Romans 8:28) and, "*For I know the thoughts that I think toward you,' says the Lord, 'thoughts of peace and not of evil, to give you a future and a hope'*" (Jeremiah 29:11). God has a purpose (and a process) whether we realize it and understand it or not. We simply have to trust Him when we cannot understand.

. . . . . . . . . . . . . . . . . . . . . . . . . . . . . . . . . . . . . .

# Bear in mind that God always has the bigger picture in mind, other than simply blessing you.

. . . . . . . . . . . . . . . . . . . . . . . . . . . . . . . . . . . . . .

Looking back in time, I can see that God even used my broken promises and situations as part of my process. Little did I know that His hand was upon me to protect me and sustain me for the process I was about to go through . . . until my hope was eventually rewarded.

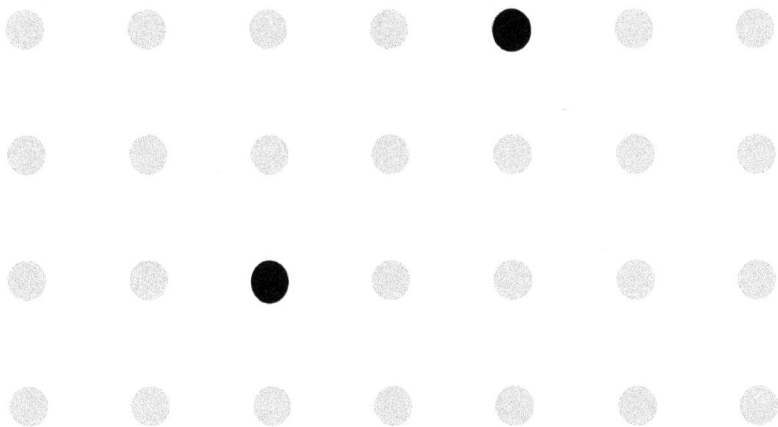

# CHAPTER 3

# GOD'S HAND IN THE JOURNEY

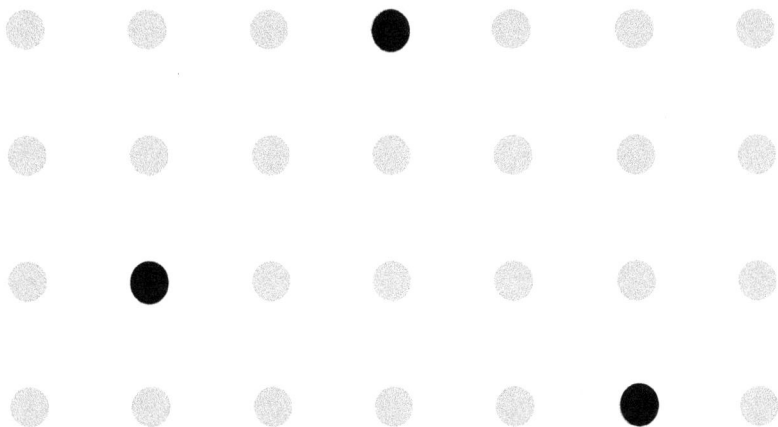

The next season in God's process for me began one morning in June of 1984. God's alarm clock suddenly rang, and I heard the bell loud and clear. I still wasn't reaching out to the Lord, but God knew how to get my attention. That day was to be the beginning of a molding process for me in which I was placed on the potter's wheel of Jeremiah 18, and God seriously began to shape my life.

June 7th seemed like just another morning for me to get up, get dressed, eat something totally unhealthy for breakfast and run out the door to work. It was the summer just before my senior year of high school, and that was my present routine. It had seemed to be going well for a time, but now that would all change.

When I woke up that day, I showered as usual, got dressed and headed toward the kitchen to eat breakfast. I didn't make it that far.

We lived in a double-wide mobile home, which most people didn't recognize as one. A hallway passed the bathroom I shared with my brother and sister and led to my room. At the other end of the hallway was the dining room where God's alarm clock suddenly went off in my life. At the time, I wanted to hit the snooze button because I didn't want to awake to what God was doing in my life.

Like having a knife penetrate my stomach and then someone twisting that knife, a pain shot through my mid-section. I had never experienced such extreme pain in all my life, pain that literally took my breath away. This pain was so severe that it caused me to collapse and pass out right in front of my mother. I hit the floor with a thud, like a sandbag hitting the ground.

Mom came across the kitchen and called my brother to help me up. She kept screaming at me, "Are you all right? Are you all right?" I could hear her frightened pleas, yet I was in so much pain that it was difficult to respond.

With my brother's help, Mom was able to get me up, and we headed straight for the door to get me to the hospital. God was up to something in my life, but I couldn't imagine what.

He had been at work, for He knows when we are about to go through trials and has a unique way of showing us that He cares. Too often, however, we miss it. I sure did on this occasion. God had made an appointment for me—a divine setup—but I missed the significance of it until later in life.

In preparation for all that was ahead, God had sent a new pastor to our small church, and he had five sons. The thing about those boys that stood out to me was that they were on fire for Jesus and cool all at the same time. To me, it always seemed that a pastor's kids were the worst kids in the church or else they were total geeks. I mean no offense by this. It was just all I had ever seen, and so this was my concept at the time.

These guys were different, really awesome. For instance, they were very musically talented and could play anything. All they had to do was hear a few notes of a song, and "boom," they could start playing it.

One particular Sunday before church, the oldest of the boys, Jamie, was playing a bass guitar and, man, he was incredible on that thing. I was listening to him warm up before the rest of the band got there, and he surprised and shocked me when he began to play a song that I knew, but it wasn't a song you would expect to hear in church. I walked up to him and asked, "Do you know what you're playing?"

His answer was no, that he didn't know exactly what he was playing; he was just playing something he had heard when a guy drove by him as he was walking to church that morning. He was playing, "Let's Hear It for the Boys" perfectly, note for note. I could have sung along with his playing just by the bass line.

Jamie had a younger brother named Keith who was equally talented and drove a Camaro, so I was trippin' over these guys who were cool and yet saved. I mean, they loved Jesus with everything in their hearts. At the high school talent show, Keith took the stage by himself and, before performing on piano, he boldly proclaimed to the entire high school student body that "Jesus hung up for their hang-ups," and they should consider giving their lives to Christ. Then he sang an old Leon Patillo song, "Star of the Morning," that totally rocked. To my surprise, everyone there exploded to their feet in applause as he finished.

Those guys took me into their home and into their lives and called me their friend. I know without question they were sent by God into my life to show me how true salvation looks, to help me put a face to Christ. They were only at our church for one year before their father took another pastorate (where he still serves today). I didn't realize it at the time, but later, as I reflected on my time with them, I realized they had molded my faith and showed me true love and salvation. God had set me up, and I didn't even know it.

· · · · · · · · · · · · · · · · · · · · · · · · · · · · · ·

I know without question they were sent by God into my life to show me how true salvation looks, to help me put a face to Christ.

· · · · · · · · · · · · · · · · · · · · · · · · · · · · · ·

This divine appointment was right on time because when this family came along, my life was about to go into a tailspin. This pain I was now feeling in my stomach was very intense and only getting worse, so Mom rushed me to the local hospital. It was a typical small-town hospital, but that was where you went when you got sick.

There was no way I could have been prepared for all the tests I was about to go through. I spent the next full week enduring test after test, after test, after yet another test, mostly what they called

GI's. Until then, I had thought the term *G.I.* meant a military man and woman, but it didn't take long for me to realize that GI's were the most uncomfortable medical tests on the planet. They were gastrointestinal (thus GI) tests, examinations of the internal organs related to food processing, primarily the esophagus, the stomach and the intestines.

After spending a couple of weeks in the hospital, I felt well again. The doctors had not yet been able to diagnose my problem, so they wanted to run a few more tests until the weekend, but when these tests also showed nothing, they finally gave up and declared me fit enough to return home.

But that first trip to the hospital would be just one of many. In the days ahead, I had to go at least two or three times a month. I would be checking in and out of the hospital until September, and all during those months the doctors had no real clue as to what was going on in my body. I don't remember them treating me for anything in particular (other than "exhaustion").

At one point, they thought I might have allergies, and I underwent a series of tests to determine if the particular symptoms I was suffering might be caused by something like that. All of the tests proved negative.

Finally, in late September of that year, I was referred to a gastroenterologist in Houston. He was highly involved in research for some of the most noted hospitals in the Houston medical field, and he immediately had me checked into Texas Children's Hospital.

At seventeen, I was possibly the oldest "kid" on my floor in that hospital, but, believe me, I *did* act like a baby when it came to pain. And I didn't weigh much more than some of the other children on that wing. At check-in and registration, I weighed in at a whopping 107 pounds.

There I was, a six-foot-tall young man, but I looked like some lab specimen for a high school science class. I'm referring to the one that stands in the corner to help you learn the names of the bones and how their structure works in the human anatomy. I was perfect for that role because the bones in my body could literally be counted. Right away this new doctor ordered up the same series of torture tests I had already endured in our local hospital.

I can never forget the frustration of the first young nurse who entered my room. Her responsibility was to place an IV in my arm, but she sadly missed the targeted vein six times. It was unfathomable to me how she could miss it because it could be seen as plain as day. (Since then I have learned from my wife, a nurse, that some veins tend to "roll"). Through all the pain of the sticking and re-sticking, I actually felt sorry for that young lady. But after I warned her that if she missed again, I would "just do without an IV," she retreated from my room and called for a replacement. This time it was the charge nurse, and trust me, this lady did not miss.

Again, God was up to something in my life, of which I was as yet totally unaware. Little did I know that I was on track for a head-on collision with God Almighty Himself!

I am amazed today at how much God loves us, even when we are ignoring Him. He miraculously worked out my parents' and grandparents' work schedules so that I had someone with me through every night I spent in that hospital. God is good and knew how to take care of a frightened seventeen-year-old boy who had somehow thought he was already a man. Friends of mine from all over the area were praying for me, even though I had not repented or prayed myself for such a long time.

Youth groups I didn't even attend were praying for me, and one of the youth pastors who was praying for me during this time is now one of my best friends. All over the country, people were praying for me, but as unbelievable as it was, that frightened hard-headed kid still had not prayed. I really don't know why I was resisting God. I had been raised in church and knew about prayer and the resulting power of God. He is so good. The Scriptures tell us that He watches over us, but we don't seem to believe it when we can't see Him or what He is up to.

Another important truth to remember is that all things *do* work together for our good, even though it is hard to believe when we can't see Him at work on our behalf. Let me help you. When you cannot see God, it does not mean He is not there. I was about to discover how very much He was there with me.

. . . . . . . . . . . . . . . . . . . . . . . . . . . . . . . . . . .

Another important truth to remember is that all things do work together for our good, even though it is hard to believe when we can't see Him at work on our behalf.

. . . . . . . . . . . . . . . . . . . . . . . . . . . . . . . . . . .

In the book of Esther in the Bible, God's name isn't mentioned a single time, yet one cannot read the book of Esther and say God wasn't present. Remember, no matter how dark your day may seem, Jesus is still a friend who *"sticks closer than a brother"* (Proverbs 18:24). He is right there with you.

I have learned over the years that when you cannot hear God speak to you, you can pick up the Bible and read Him in His Word. The Word of God is God's love letter and Jesus' last will and testament to us, so we know the heart of the Savior through it. I tell people all the time that when the circumstances of life are making it impossible to hear from the Lord, they should open the Word of God and read God on its pages.

The tests that had to be repeated were even more uncomfortable this time. One particular test involved having dye injected into my veins, and this caused me to experience severe burning and convulsions.

Another time, during a GI series I was receiving, the doctor would tell an assistant to pump, but it was so painful that I would beg them to stop. This went on until I had my fill and actually took a swing at him. By that time, I was convinced that if he was going to cause me that much pain, I was going to get my shot in on him as well.

I drew back to hit him squarely in the nose, but missed and, unfortunately, hit a young lady in the jaw. Her only job had been to stand there and make sure my head was comfortable, and like a nut, I had hit her.

My grandfather, who had been observing our progress through a window in the door, broke into the room at that moment. He wanted (1) To help bring me under control, and (2) To insist that the test be stopped for the moment. He had watched me go through enough pain for one day and wasn't about to tolerate any more, especially since I had been yelling "STOP"! I feel bad for that lady I hit to this day, but at least the tests were stopped!

That afternoon the doctor came in for what I assumed was his usual visit, but this time, he asked to speak to my parents alone outside of my room. I got very nervous about this pow-wow because I was not included. What was the man telling my parents that he didn't want me to hear?

The door to my room hadn't closed totally, and I found that I was able to overhear everything that was said. I believe God orchestrated that situation as well. The doctor was informing my parents that he was recommending my transfer the following day to the M.D. Anderson Cancer Center.

Having grown up in the Houston area, I knew the name M.D. Anderson Center. It was one of the greatest cancer hospitals in the world, and when I heard it, fear shot through my body like a lightning bolt.

The bad news was about to get worse. My parents didn't know that I had overheard them, and when they walked back into the room, they made every effort to be positive and upbeat. But then their bombshell fell: they would both have to leave for the night to return home to check on my brother and sister and to gather additional clothing for the move the next day. Even worse, my grandparents would not be able to stay the night with me either. It was to be my first night ever to stay alone in the hospital since the onset of my illness. God was setting me up much like He had Jacob in the Bible.

Jacob was a conniving fellow who had stolen his brother Esau's birthright and then run away to live with his equally-crooked uncle. But God led Jacob to a face-to-face encounter with himself. Sometimes we don't need an encounter with anyone except ourselves. We need to look at our lives realistically and honestly to discover the real us. It may be scary, but if we get honest with who we are, God will get real with us about who He is.

Jacob went to a river called Jabbok, which meant "poured out" or "emptied." We all need to face a Jabbok, if Jesus is to be Lord of our lives. It is a fearful thing to pour out all of who we are to the Lord, but the night Jacob wrestled with the Angel of the Lord, it forever changed his life.

The Angel asked Jacob, "Who are you?" and Jacob had to admit who he was. The name *Jacob* means "trickster, deceiver, conniver," and "nothing good." Sometimes, when we come to our own personal Jabbok, our place of pouring out, we can see who we really are. This gives God a chance to rename us.

The Angel of the Lord told Jacob that from then on, he would be known as Israel, meaning "Prince with God." He said, *"Thy name shall be called no more Jacob, but Israel: for as a prince hast thou power with God and with men, and hast prevailed"* (Genesis 32:28, KJV). When we get real with Jesus, He will call us by what He sees, not how we actually are or how anyone else may try to define us. (The full story of Jacob's struggle for identity is found in chapters 27–32.)

Left alone on October 9th, 1984, I encountered the moment of my personal Jabbok. I was suddenly alone with all my fears and concerns, having overheard the bad news that I would be leaving the next morning for M.D. Anderson, to begin the search for cancer in my body. Those were my thoughts and fears.

By five o'clock that evening, the IV tubes had been removed, and even the hospital staff was not checking on me as often as they had before. Now I felt so completely alone. I tried to watch some television and tried anything and everything else I could think of to keep my mind occupied, but no matter what I did, there was no denying the haunting thought that I was going to die of cancer.

It is amazing to me how the devil knows how and when to jump on the bandwagon when everything around appears to be falling apart, but if we will look for God in those most trying moments and have hope in Him, He will show up for us.

As I lay there in bed, with all of my thoughts and anxieties, I opened the drawer of the nightstand next to my bed and, to my wonder and surprise, there was a Bible placed there by the Gideons. (Gideons International is a ministry which distributes Bibles all over the world, in foreign countries, as well as in American schools, hospitals, nursing homes and many other places. I regularly support this organization, and you will soon see why.) As I looked at the Bible, many thoughts I had as a child came rushing back to my mind. Teddy's house became real to me all over again, my camp experience and many of the sermons I had ever heard began to flood my mind and heart, and I started to weep. I grabbed that Bible, clutched it with my arms to my chest, and prayed a simple little prayer: "God, if You are real, I need to know it; and I need to know it now." Immediately, the door to my room swung open, but no one was there. Still, I could feel Someone in the room with me.

Have you ever experienced the feeling of someone watching you, yet you could not see a single soul? That's how I felt that night. I quickly closed my eyes, for I knew Jesus had entered my hospital room.

Once, when I was a kid, I had heard a preacher say that no one could see God and live. Certain that I was not ready to die, I now squeezed my eyes shut as tightly as possible, so as not to see God and have to die.

Then I felt Him walk around my bed, and fear overtook me. At the same time, I felt such an unexplainable peace.

Next, the strangest thing happened, for I felt the form of a hand laid firmly on my chest. This feeling was so detailed that I could feel each finger and the thumb touching me. The really unique thing was that this hand was directly under the Bible, which I still had clenched tightly to my chest.

Then the Lord spoke. This was not a still, small voice or even Him speaking in my spirit. Rather, God spoke out loud to me. It sounded like waves crashing on the jetties during a rough sea, and yet His voice was as peaceful and clear as a bird singing on a clear, spring day.

I have never heard the Lord speak audibly to me in that way again. He has spoken to me through His Word, through other people and, at times, through certain circumstances, but not audibly.

Because that happened, I have never believed that I was more special than others. I just had a hard head. God shouldn't have to do the extreme to get our attention, but often He does the extreme, as He did for me, because He loves us so much. My goal and desire these days is that I would be so in tune with His still, small voice, which He speaks into my heart, that He will not have to speak to me audibly again until the day He says, "Well done, good and faithful servant."

How amazing! The Lord came into my hospital room and spoke to me as a teenager, and, in doing so, He called my name. He said, "Donald, . . ." Isn't it good to know that God knows your name and where you are in life? It doesn't matter who you are and where you are, God knows your name, and He knows how to rescue you if you will just call out to His Son, Jesus.

On that first Easter morning, Mary thought Jesus was the gardener . . . until He called her by name. When Jesus calls your name, there is no mistaking Who is calling.

God spoke audibly to me that day, "Donald, you are my child, and in the palm of my hand; everything is going to be all right. Do not be afraid."

And that was it! I felt his hand lift from my chest, and the door opened and closed again. By now, my eyes were open, and again I did not see anyone, but I knew God had been in the room with me and had spoken to me. That night, I slept more peacefully than I had in months. I knew everything was going to be all right. I was expecting to be healed, and so I had a renewed hope.

The Bible says, *"For where your treasure is, there your heart will be also"* (Matthew 6:21). Faith and hope reside in our hearts. So where is your treasure? It's where your heart is. If your heart is in the hand of God, then you can hope in God. If your heart is in the things of this life, your hope will rise and fall with the ebb and flow of current circumstances.

Hope must also be tested. Faith, hope, and love are all like a rubber band. They are useless until they are stretched and wrapped around something. You don't know if you have faith until you are in the middle of a good fight. Trouble is an opportunity to demonstrate faith, and it is the same with hope and love.

> Faith, hope, and love are all like a rubber band. They are useless until they are stretched and wrapped around something.

Hope shows up in the middle of trouble, at least the God-kind of hope does. I was in the middle of a fight for my life, and hope suddenly showed up. I suddenly knew that God was going to turn things around for me.

Faith said I had His Word on it. As noted earlier, "Faith is *the substance of things hoped for*," so, based on God's Word, I had an expected end that was different from where I currently was. I knew my current circumstances did not represent the end of me. I was going to come through this to the other side.

Hope and faith are the reason Joseph kept such a positive attitude, though he was in the pit, though he was in Potiphar's house, with the woman lying about him. He went to prison, but he never got despondent. He never got discouraged because he had a dream and a word. His circumstance didn't yet line up with the vision and dream God had given him, so he knew it was not yet the end.

I had more than a dream; I had an audible declaration from God. I knew God was going to move me to the next place. It was only a matter of time.

The next morning the doctor exploded into my room, again asking for my parents. He said he had some news he wanted to share with them. I thought to myself, "Doc, you sent them home last night, so they could get clothes and send me to M.D. Anderson, and so they left me here all alone." I didn't say it, but I surely thought it.

"What news do you have, Doc?" I anxiously inquired.

He replied, "I have to wait until your parents arrive, but I do have some good news for you."

You don't tell a seventeen-year-old that and then not tell him what the good news is. That is cruel and unusual punishment.

After what seemed to be an eternity (but was only about an hour), my parents arrived. For an anxious young man who had just spent the evening with the Lord Jesus Himself, I was ready to hear the news that I had been healed. The doctor began by doing the ole' "good-news-bad-news" routine. I just wanted him to speak. Simply tell me the news, man.

Finally, he got around to it: "Mr. and Mrs. Gibson, about nine o'clock last evening, while reviewing your son's case, I came across some x-rays taken back in the hospital in Sweeny," the doctor began. He placed the x-rays in question on the lighted screen, so we could all see them clearly (or as clearly as x-rays can be seen by a layperson).

Then he continued: "The good news is that we now know what is wrong with your son. Do you see this discoloration in his ileum, between the small and large intestine?" My parents agreed that they could see it, so I went along with them, even though it all looked like a blur to me.

The doctor continued, "This is our problem. Your son has Crohn's disease. The bad news is we don't know what causes it or how to cure it, but we can treat it with high doses of steroids called Prednisone."

Wow! Crohn's disease. What was that? I, for one, had never heard of it. We all had a lot to learn.

Since my diagnosis in the early 1980's, there has been much progress and research accomplished concerning this disease. Still, there is no known cure. As noted in the front matter of the book, according to Wikipedia:

*"Crohn's disease is an inflammatory disease of the intestines that may affect any part of the gastrointestinal tract, causing a wide variety of symptoms. It primarily causes abdominal pain, diarrhea, vomiting or weight loss, but may also cause complications outside of the gastrointestinal tract such as skin rashes, arthritis and inflammation of the eyes. Being an auto-immune disease in which the body's immune system attacks the gastrointestinal tract causing inflammation, it is classified as a type of inflammatory bowel disease. There is no known pharmaceutical or surgical cure for Crohn's disease. Treatment options are restricted to controlling symptoms, maintaining remission, and preventing relapse."*[2]

Instead of going to M.D. Anderson Cancer Center that next morning, I was released with a bottle of Prednisone pills with instructions to take 120 mg. a day for a certain amount of time and then, eventually, to begin to taper off the dosage. I found out later that Prednisone has two to three pages listed in the medical journals of possible harmful side-effects associated with it. But that day, as I left Texas Children's Hospital in Houston and returned home to good ole' Sweeny, I expected to be completely healed. After all, God had come into my room, spoken audibly to me, and placed His hand on me. Surely I was well.

I followed the doctor's orders and took the pills, and I quickly bloated up to a size I had never been before or since. I had checked into the hospital at 107 lbs, but after taking those pills for a short

2 "Crohn's Disease," Wikipedia (Wikimedia Foundation), https://en.wikipedia.org/wiki/Crohn%27s_disease.

period of time, I weighed 183. They caused me to blow up like a toad. For me, that was not good, but then, as the doctor had prescribed, we began to taper off the steroids, until I was eventually no longer on the drugs, and I was able to get back down to a normal weight.

But I just knew I was healed, so drugs or no drugs, it didn't matter. God had said that I was in His hand, so naturally that meant I was completely well, healed and had no trouble, right? Not on your life—or mine. I was about to learn one of the greatest lessons in the world—how to continue trusting God and His promises in spite of your current negative circumstances.

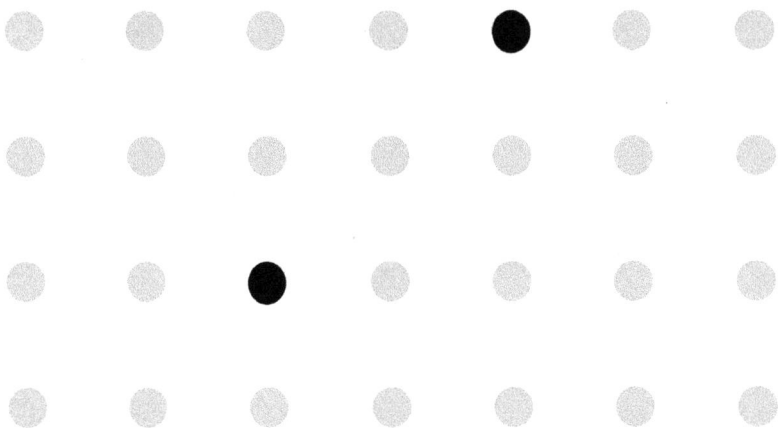

# CHAPTER 4

# LEARNING TO TRUST

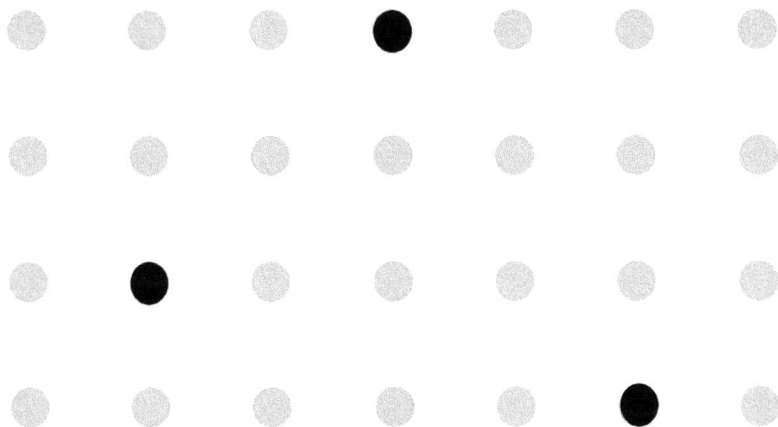

One of the passages of scripture that helped me in my times of suffering was Matthew 11:1–6:

*Now it came to pass, that He departed from there to teach and to preach in their cities. And when John had heard in prison about the works of Christ, he sent two of his disciples and said to Him, "Are You the Coming One, or do we look for another?"*

*Jesus answered and said to them, "Go and tell John the things which you hear and see: the blind see and the lame walk; the lepers are cleansed and the deaf hear; the dead are raised up and the poor have the gospel preached to them. And blessed is he who is not offended because of Me."*

The truths found in this passage became profoundly valuable for my life at the time and, still today, I find them equally valuable, if not more so.

This is something to be considered: John the Baptist was sending men to Jesus with questions, doubts, insecurities and real fears. John was the same guy who had declared to the people of Israel, *"Behold the lamb of God who takes away the sin of the world"* (John 1:29). He was the same guy who had baptized Jesus, saw the Holy Ghost descend on Him in the form of a dove and heard the heavenly Father say, *"This is My beloved Son, in whom I am well pleased"*

(Matthew 3:17). This was the same John the Baptist, the bold preacher who ate locust and wild honey and wasn't afraid of anyone, but now he was filled with questions: *"Are you the one or do we look for another?"*

What John was really asking Jesus that day was this: "If You are really the Son of God, the Lamb who will take away the sins of the world, why am I imprisoned and why will I be executed?" And this was my dilemma too: I had heard God's voice and felt His touch, and so why was I still sick?

Was it God's fault? Was it my fault? Surely someone had to be at fault. But no, not really. It is not about fault; it is simply about trust. Like John, the Lord was asking me if I could trust Him and not be offended.

Jesus loved John (who was His earthly cousin), and He used the next several verses in Matthew 11 to brag on John, to tell everyone how great a man of God John really was, and yet in spite of all that, John was still in prison and he would eventually lose his life for his bold denunciation of sin. John's circumstances, however, did not change God's love for him one bit.

We often need to ask ourselves if we get offended at Christ when He doesn't come through for us *when and how* we think He should. The Scriptures say, *"Blessed is he who is not offended because of Me"* (Matthew 11:6). We cannot afford to be offended at God because He doesn't do "when," "where," "how" and "what" we think He should. He isn't our genie; He is God, our Father.

. . . . . . . . . . . . . . . . . . . . . . . . . . . . . . . .

We often need to ask ourselves if
we get offended at Christ when
He doesn't come through for us
when and how we think He should.

. . . . . . . . . . . . . . . . . . . . . . . . . . . . . . . .

I had to settle the question once and for all in my heart that I wasn't going to be mad at God. Sometimes that is hard, but I have learned to tell Him in prayer when I am mad at Him or when I think I have gotten the short end of the stick. He understands and still loves me, especially when I am honest with Him and with myself.

Thankfully, the doctors were able to manage the Crohn's disease with medication for the moment. From time to time, I would have great struggles with it, and at other times, I would feel perfectly well. There is one thing to remember in all of this: I was in a PROCESS that was for a greater purpose than just my personal physical well-being. God was preparing me for ministry, ministry in the midst of my misery.

Anyone can minister from a lofty position of status or health or when everything seems to be coming together, but can we minister through our own pain? When I gave my life to the Lord at the age of seven, I knew God had a purpose for my life, although I never imagined it would be in ministry. I aspired to be an accountant or a school teacher. (A good pastor should be able to do a little of both.)

Then, one Sunday evening, when I was still seventeen, after returning home from one of the many long ordeals in the hospital, I responded to an altar call my pastor gave. I simply went to the front to pray and seek the Lord, with no particular sin to confess at the moment (or at least I couldn't think of any). I'm sure someone else could have come up with a few for me, but I just went forward to pray specifically about my future. I was a senior in high school, with a load of decisions ahead of me.

During that time in my life, my best friend and I would meet at the church every morning to pray. Before you begin to think I was really spiritual, let me interject that often our pastor would come in and wake us up and tell us we were going to be late for school. Nonetheless, we were attempting to seek after God's purpose for our lives. I am so glad that if we simply make an attempt to pursue God, He goes the extra distance and pursues us, no matter our shortcomings. So, on that particular Sunday, I was doing what I normally would do. I went to the altar to pray for direction.

There was no big fanfare, no lights, no thundering voice, simply a still, small whisper in my heart saying, "You will declare My Word to people, and many will be saved." That is what I heard in my heart and mind. I knew the voice of God, so I knew at that moment God was calling me to ministry.

This experience wasn't earth-shattering to me at the moment, but when I got back to my seat, I told my mom that the Lord had just called me into the ministry, and she got very excited about it and began to weep and shout at the same time. It was as if the Lord had called *her* to the ministry and not me. Actually, He had. My parents have always been two of the biggest supporters of my ministry, and I never would have been able to follow God fully without their love and support.

I had planned to meet the next day with an Army recruiter and a Navy recruiter at school. My dad had served in the Navy and, still being confused about my future, I thought I would too. By morning, I had reasoned away the call of God on my life, and I went on to meet with the recruiters.

But that next night, after I had gone to bed, I had the strangest dream. I dreamed that I was in an inspection line for new military recruits. I was standing there in my shorts and a T-shirt, much like you see on television, when suddenly a voice came over an intercom system asking the question, "Donald, what are you doing in this line when you were called to preach the Word of God?"

Nervously, I spoke to the voice and said that if I could be shown how to get out of the line, I would. Immediately, a man dressed in all white tapped me on the shoulder and commanded me to go through a certain door. As I walked through that door, I woke up with a scripture on my mind. It was from the prophet Isaiah:

*But now, thus says the LORD, who created you, O Jacob,*
*And He who formed you, O Israel:*
*"Fear not, for I have redeemed you;*
*I have called you by your name;*
*You are Mine.*
*When you pass through the waters, I will be with you;*
*And through the rivers, they shall not overflow you.*
*When you walk through the fire, you shall not be burned,*
*Nor shall the flame scorch you.*
*For I am the LORD your God,*
*The Holy One of Israel, your Savior."*
Isaiah 43:1–3

That promise was now mine, and there would be no military career for me.

Ephesians 4:23–24 tells us: *"and be renewed in the spirit of your mind, and that you put on the new man which was created according to God, in true righteousness and holiness."* God will put us in a place where He can begin to transform us. But that place is not really a place at all. Rather, it is a person—the Lord Jesus. We have been placed in Christ.

When we ask Jesus to come into our hearts, He doesn't just come into us. We also go into Him. And being placed in Christ provides for us a sufficiency for everything we need.

But there is more: God also places us in the Body of Christ. Each of us has a place and a purpose in His Body. I had now been called to that Body to be a pastor. I could not plan my future: my future was already planned for me.

. . . . . . . . . . . . . . . . . . . . . . . . . . . . . . . . .

# Each of us has a place and a purpose in His Body.

. . . . . . . . . . . . . . . . . . . . . . . . . . . . . . . . .

I had a very unusual experience the following Sunday. Our church regularly had visitors, and this Sunday was no different. One of the visitors that particular Sunday was an elderly lady. Her hair was as white as snow, and she was wearing an off-white colored dress, so that as she came striding into the service, she glowed like an angel. (At least that's what I thought an angel would look like.) She was probably in her late sixties or early seventies, and only about 5 feet 2 inches in height. Nevertheless, she had a presence and grace about her that captivated me.

As soon as worship began, I forgot about her because I was there to worship the Lord. Then, all of sudden, I had the feeling that someone was looking at me. Well, not just looking at me, but standing right in front of me.

I had my eyes closed in worship, and I was afraid to open them, but then I felt a gentle tap on my chest. I opened my eyes, and when I did, that angelic-like lady was standing face-to-face with me.

Pointing her finger straight in my face, she declared, "You are like a frog. . . . God will lead you all the days of your life and ministry . . . but you will have to jump before the lily pad appears, for your walk and ministry will be one of faith." And with that, she turned around and returned to her seat. It took me a while to process that, but I liked it.

This woman of God became a member of our church and a good friend of my mother and, over time, I began to build a relationship with her. She became Sister Showers to me, and she had a huge impact on my life and ministry, often speaking keywords into my life.

Those very first words Sister Showers spoke into my life were right on. Throughout my entire ministry, I have had to take leaps of faith, like a frog. This book is one of those leaps, and I can tell you that it has been the greatest ride of a lifetime. Because I have been willing to leap by faith, God has blessed me in areas I would have never imagined and probably would never have experienced otherwise. From the day she gave that word, I have never looked back.

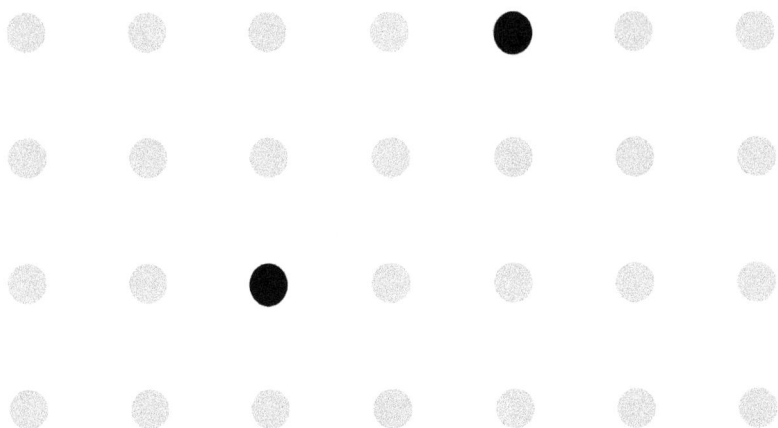

# CHAPTER 5

# A SEASON OF SOWING

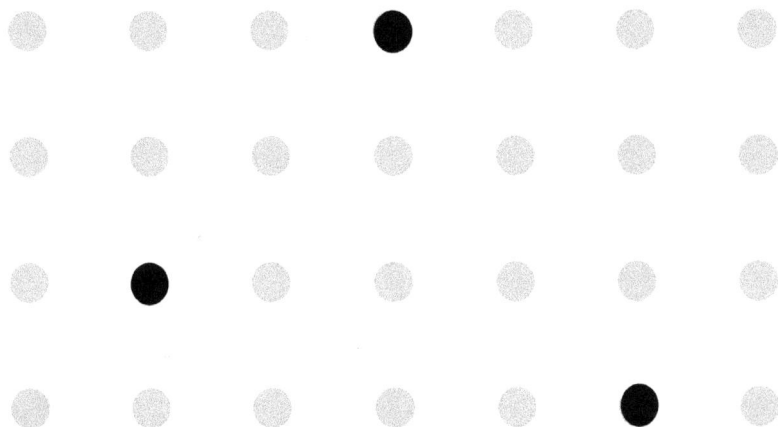

My part-time ministry began almost immediately, just two weeks after that dream, there at our small church in Sweeny. The Lord allowed me to get a glimpse of the reality of the scripture which declares, *"by His stripes we are healed"* (Isaiah 53:5).

Nine months to a year had passed since my encounter with the Lord in the hospital. The pastor with the five sons had moved on, and we now had a new pastor. This pastor, noting my sincerity and my passion for God, allowed me to begin leading worship. That particular day I was leading, and we were singing the old hymn, "Nothing But the Blood of Jesus." Suddenly I was inspired to boldly declare that Jesus took stripes on His back so that we might be healed, and I began to call out the names of people in the church who were sick and have them come forward for prayer. Right before my eyes, God began to heal everyone I prayed for. Wow! God was answering my prayers for the sick.

So I did what any other man of faith and power would do: I laid my hands on my own head, because I wanted Him to heal me that day too. Instead, the Lord launched me into a season in which I prayed for other people and saw them miraculously touched by God and healed, while I remained sick in my own body.

God isn't cruel or unconcerned, but the question remains to be answered: can we sow seeds of faith and healing into someone else's life, while ours is in shambles? The Scriptures say, *"Whatsoever a man soweth, that shall he also reap"* (Galatians 6:7, KJV). Why do we so often relegate this truth to money, and not also to faith, healing, kindness, grace and a number of other worthy seeds that need to be sown into the lives of other believers, as well as non-believers?

- - - - - - - - - - - - - - - - - - - - - - - - - - - - -

God isn't cruel or unconcerned, but the question remains to be answered: can we sow seeds of faith and healing into someone else's life, while ours is in shambles?

Thus, my journey of bringing healing and seeking to be healed began. I went everywhere I heard good things were happening to have people pray for me for healing. Especially during the times I was in great pain, I sought out any man or woman of God who might be able to touch Him on my behalf, so that my circumstances could change.

Desperate times call for desperate measures. I would sometimes fast by choice, while at other times I had no choice at all. I was just too sick to eat. I needed a miracle, and I was desperate for God to do the work.

I asked every minister who came to our church to pray for me to be healed. I went to other meetings, revivals and camp meetings, hoping God would heal me, but I remained ill.

In our journeys as Christians, each of us is either going into a trial, coming out of a trial or we are actually still in the trial. Therefore standing on the Word of God and maintaining hope are essential parts of the Christian walk. We need to be prepared for whatever circumstances come our way, and we must be armed with the knowledge of God in how to deal with them. That requires a steady hope.

I have learned that there are three things that will quickly kill your hope:

1) **Looking at only your circumstances will kill hope.** If you have hope in an expected end or you have hope in a dream, then you have an anticipation of what God is going to do. Therefore, you cannot look at your present circumstances. Sooner or later, you must let Jesus' promise rise up in you so that you speak to your mountain about how big your God is, instead of concentrating on how big your mountain is. Jesus said: "... *if you have faith as a mustard seed, you will say to this mountain, 'Move from here to there,' and it will move; and nothing will be impossible for you*" (Matthew 17:20). If you look at your circumstances only, you will go crazy. Here

I was laying hands on other people and seeing them healed, yet I remained ill. If I had focused only on my illness, I would never have fulfilled God's will in my life.

2) **Doubting God's promises concerning you will kill hope.** If you have received a promise, take it to the bank and cash it. Don't give up on it. God's promises are *"yea"* and *"amen"* (2 Corinthians 1:20). You have to take your hands off of the situation and say, "God, You've got a big problem on Your hands. You've got to come through." When you get to that point, God says, "Good! Now I have you right where I want you, because if you would have come through with your hands on it, you would have tried to take the credit." Even in the midst of the trial, hope in God and keep your hope in Him. If you don't, if you fail to stand on His promise for your life, if you fail to stand on the Word, the enemy will start to erode your hope, and eventually, he will erode your faith, and you will say, "I guess I never really heard from God." God had promised me healing, and I was determined to see it come to pass, whatever else happened.

3) **Ceasing to speak God's promises will kill hope.** If the enemy can shut your mouth concerning your promise, he can impact your hope and shake your faith. Like David, you must encourage yourself in the Lord (see 1 Samuel 30:6). Speak God's promises aloud and let them cause you to rise up above your circumstances.

If you want to kill hope in your life, only look at your circumstances, doubt what God has said about you and stop speaking His promises. If, on the other hand, you want to maintain hope and have trust in God, take a lesson from Abraham. He believed God's word about having a baby and kept believing it for twenty-five years. After those many years of hoping and trusting in God's promise, Abraham and Sarah finally had their miracle baby.

Through this process, Abraham didn't do everything right. He put his hands on God's promise and ended up with Ishmael (see Genesis 16). If we are to put our trust in the Lord, we can't cast away the promise God gave us, no matter what we have to go through. We must keep declaring God's Word and His personal promises to us.

Too many people place their hopes in what they see and in this world instead of in God. But God is the source of all hope, and therefore our hope must be in Him. Don't put your hope in people, for even people with the very best intentions will often let you down.

## Too many people place their hopes in what they see and in this world instead of in God.

Sometimes we think God Himself has let us down because He doesn't work when we think He should. Know this: God will never let you down. If there is some delay in His action, the purpose of that delay may be to work out some "stuff" in you.

While I was in part-time ministry in Sweeny, I met a young lady I had known in the past, but now I was greatly attracted to her, and we began to date. I thought it was amazing that she would date me.

Jonna and I had met a couple of years earlier when she was dating a friend of mine. Our two youth groups would often meet at a local pizza restaurant. The first time she met me, I was standing on the roof of a car yelling at someone across the parking lot. She asked my friend, "Who is the crazy guy on the car?" To which my friend replied, "That's Donald! He's my friend!" It definitely wasn't love at first sight. That's for sure.

As it turned out, Jonna and my friend weren't that serious about each other, and that year he went off to college (as did I), so I lost contact with her. Then, in the winter of 1987, our area youth ministry put on an all-night bowling event, and because I was back in town, I attended. I had left Bible college and gone back home to attend the local junior college, to work and save some money while I continued to study. Jonna also attended that all-night bowling event, along with her youth group, her brother and one of her sisters, and I struck up a conversation with her. To my surprise, she didn't run away from me, and we literally sat there and talked all night long. As it turned out, we had a lot in common and shared many of the same interests.

The event was over when the sun came up, but Jonna and I decided to go have breakfast together and continue our conversation. Over breakfast, we decided to go on a date. That "date" would be to go running with her and her brother.

Jonna and her brother were cross-country runners at their high school, and it so happened that I had also run cross-country when I was in school. But that had been three years before, and I probably had not run a hundred yards since then (because of my sickness). But it's amazing what you can do when you're trying to impress a beautiful blonde-haired, brown-eyed girl.

Actually, in the back of my mind, I had thought we might walk together a little, like you see in romantic movies, but oh, no, Jonna and her brother were serious about their running, so when the time came, we all took off.

To them, it was just a jog, but to me, it seemed like a sprint, and within a quarter of a mile, I needed a second wind. Still, I was determined to put forth my best effort. Jonna had to know I was dying, but I was doing my best not to show it.

In what seemed like an eternity, I finally persuaded her to walk for a few minutes, and I took the opportunity to confess that I hadn't run in many years—three to be exact, I confessed. Somehow I believe this had been painfully obvious to her all along. But we had a blast that day, running, walking and just talking.

In the midst of me gasping for breath and wondering when this "fun" run was going to be over, we made the decision to go out again, this time to Fame City, an amusement park in Houston. We went with her sister and brother-in-law.

When I went to pick Jonna up at her house, I had to meet her parents, you know the awkward-meet-the-parents deal, and I was in for a shock. I had heard of things like this happening but never expected them to ever happen to me. Jonna's dad met me at the door. He was six foot one and weighed about 240 pounds, and it was all muscle. That was intimidating enough, but he was also holding a double-barreled ten gauge shotgun in his hands. With that, he really didn't have to say a word. His point was already well taken.

Can you imagine it? Here I was six feet tall and 140 pounds tops, and he told me to come in and take a seat and then he began to interrogate me, all the while holding the shotgun across his lap. Where was I going with his daughter? What were my intentions with her? What was my true relationship with the Lord?

Years later, we were able to laugh about that night. The gun hadn't been loaded, and he hadn't even known where the shells for it were. Still, I think the only reason he said yes that night was because Jonna's sister and brother-in-law were going along with us. The last thing he said to me, as we were going out the door, was, "Keep both hands on the steering wheel." Holding the image of him with that shotgun in his hands fully in my mind, that's exactly where my hands stayed the rest of the night.

This was what I call a real first date. Fame City had everything, putt-putt golf, bowling, arcade, bumper cars, movie theatre . . . you name it, and they had it. We first went to dinner at Spaghetti Warehouse, and then it was on to Fame City. We were having a blast.

I recall asking Jonna several times during the evening if we should start for home or what time we needed to be home, to which she replied, "Oh, it doesn't matter because my sister and brother-in-law are with us." I hadn't had a curfew in years, so for me to be out late was no big deal, but for her to be out late was a different story, even if her sister and brother-in-law were along.

When we got back to her house that night, I gave her a hug. (We had gone out for several months before I finally built up the courage to kiss her.) But then, when I looked at the clock, I saw that it was 3 o'clock in the morning. Yes, her sister and brother-in-law had been with us, but, come to find out, that didn't matter as much to her parents as she had thought it would. Needless to say, we didn't go out for a couple of weeks after that because Jonna was grounded, and I was labeled a "punk kid."

Bringing their daughter home at 3 A.M. on our first official date was not the only reason for this label. There was more: I drove a black Grand-Prix with blacked-out windows, had a stereo system that had twelve speakers, two punch Rockford Fosgate amps, and I loved Christian rock music. As a matter of fact, you would hear me coming long before you saw me.

On another occasion, Jonna's mother got in my car to take it to the store (because I had parked behind her), and I had forgotten to turn down the radio. I had been listening to (or should I say jamming to) "To Hell With the Devil" by Stryper. Before long, she came back in asking if I would help her because she couldn't figure out how to turn the radio down. That was not a good way to make an impression, so I volunteered to go to the store for her.

When Jonna's grounding ended, we continued dating. We had a great time doing things together, but for a time, she had no idea how sick I was. It was one of those seasons in which my health had been doing relatively well, but that could change very quickly, and one night it did. I'll never forget that night or how the secret of my sickness came crashing to the forefront.

We had been to a dinner and a movie, and I was dropping her off at home. She invited me in to watch some television with her and her parents, and I took her up on her invitation. After watching a little television with the family, I suddenly felt an attack coming on. Quickly offering my apologies, I tried to make my way to the door, but before I could make it outside, I doubled over in severe pain and ended up on the floor in a fetal position at their front door.

This was very embarrassing for me, but I also felt sorry for Jonna and her parents because they were in such shock seeing me in this condition. In time, the pain subsided, and I went back to the living room and began to explain to them the facts of my sickness, also explaining what had just happened. It was to be one of many episodes that would take place while we were dating.

Interestingly enough, Jonna never once got rattled or spooked when this happened, and she didn't even seem to be embarrassed when it happened out in public. She would just patiently sit by me and take care of me until the pain had subsided.

The night I had planned to ask Jonna if she would marry me was an amazing evening. I had planned the whole thing in detail. Both of our houses were close to the Gulf of Mexico, so I decided that we would go have a great seafood dinner, and then I would take her to the beach and propose. Always remembering the ten gauge shotgun, I had asked her father's permission in advance to do this, and he surprised me by saying yes.

Jonna and I went to a restaurant that we both enjoyed, and then we drove to the beach. I suggested that we get out and take a walk on the beach. It was a beautiful evening, and the moon and stars were out. It was March of 1988. As we walked down the beach talking, I stopped her and got on one knee to propose. Instead of asking her to marry me, I asked her if she would like "to do life together" as my wife. I don't remember where I got that line, but all I know is that it worked. She said yes! Then we rushed home so she could tell her mom and dad. It was the second greatest choice I ever made in life, the greatest being my choice of salvation in Jesus Christ.

Jonna and I dated about two years and then got married. One night while we were still dating, we attended a revival service in her church, and Jonna and I went to the altar to have an evangelist pray for us. When he did this, the power of God came down on us in such a manner that we could not stand. We both hit the floor under the power of God. What I didn't know that night was the Lord was healing my future wife. Jonna had been told that she would never be able to have children. Later, when we were married and she became pregnant with our first-born son, Trey, I knew God had healed Jonna the night of the revival. God is at work many times, and we fail to recognize it.

After we were married, miracles increased in our ministry. I began to see people with diabetes healed. Deaf ears opened, and back problems were healed. Then one night God did a greater miracle.

We had a guest speaker that night, a young candidate, trying out to become our next pastor. During the service, one of the senior ladies of the church got up to go out and collapsed. One of the members sitting close to her was a registered nurse, and she rushed to her aid. She began checking the elder lady's vital signs and, at the same time, called for someone to dial 911.

The young preacher came down from the pulpit to encourage all the people to pray together. No sooner had he made the plea for prayer than the nurse declared that the collapsed lady had died. Undeterred, the young pastor, along with several of the church ladies and myself, began to call on the Lord fervently to intervene. In just a few moments, the elderly lady gasped for breath, and the nurse, looking white as a ghost, screamed, "She's alive again!" I saw it with my own eyes and was thus witness to a woman being raised from the dead.

I was seeing miracles in my personal life as well as the ministry, but I was still wrestling with periodic trips to the hospital during bouts of great pain, anguish and torture from my own disease.

After about a year of marriage, Jonna and I entered into full-time ministry as youth pastors in a town in South Texas named Pleasanton. Placed in our first full-time staff positions, we were blessed to serve under Pastor Larry Jones (whom I affectionately called Pastor J). He had been my pastor when I was just eleven.

Pastor J was and remains my spiritual father in the faith. He understood my sickness and graciously gave me an opportunity to participate in ministry in spite of it. There is no way he could have comprehended the severity of the pain I suffered periodically, but he gave me a chance and mentored me in ministry. I may never have gone into full-time ministry if it were not for him.

The opportunity to enter full-time ministry came about one day when Pastor J came to Sweeny to visit. While we were driving down the road toward my parents' home, he asked me a question that got my attention and pierced my heart. He simply asked, "Are you ready to get into full-time ministry?" Even though I was frightened by the prospect, two weeks later all of our belongings were in a truck headed to Pleasanton to work with my spiritual father.

There is no better way to start in full-time ministry, I promise, than to work with someone you know loves you, even as they are correcting you. Those were awesome times in Pleasanton, as the Lord did great things in our lives and ministry. When we arrived there, the church youth group consisted of only a few, but before long, it grew to a weekly attendance of more than seventy young people. It was the biggest thing going on in the whole town.

It was in that place where our eldest son was born, and there I matured in ministry, still periodically wrestling with Crohn's disease. I did my best to fulfill the work of the ministry although sometimes I was debilitated by various severe complications.

In 1992, we left Pleasanton, with the encouragement and blessing of my spiritual dad. He saw greater things ahead in my life and felt that I needed to be in a larger church. God, he said, was about to do unbelievable things in our personal lives and in our ministry. Only a true father would speak to your future and release you into what the Lord has for you, when it would be better for him to hold on to you. I love and appreciate the fact that it wasn't about Pastor Jones' ministry, but about the plan and purpose of God in our lives.

We now assumed the youth pastor's position in Mesquite, Texas, under Pastor William F. Sipes. Once again, God's favor was upon our lives and ministry and growth continued to take place.

One Sunday, Pastor Sipes had a guest speaker at the church, Brother Everitt Fjordbak. Brother Fjordbak was one of the most authentic, yet peculiar ministers I had ever met. He introduced me to the prophetic voice of God like I had never known it before. He spoke a prophetic word into my life which is still in operation today. (The writing of this book was included in that word.) At that time, the prophetic wasn't the latest catch phrase it has become today.

Brother Fjordbak blessed us with two services that Sunday, morning and evening. During the evening service, things got really interesting. Following the worship service, I took my place on the front row where I normally sat. When Brother Fjordbak took the platform, he called me back and informed me that I would be praying for the sick that night, so I needed to be anointed with oil beforehand, and he proceeded to anoint me with oil while praying over me.

Of course, I had been anointed with oil before, but never like this. He first anointed my ears and prayed, "God, let him hear every word You speak." Then he anointed and prayed for my eyes, saying, "Father, let him see from Your perspective. Give him eyes to see the things You see." By that time, I was thinking to myself: *Wow! This is different!* He went on praying and anointed my hands, my feet and my head (for my mind to be anointed).

Next, the strangest thing happened. That elder statesman of the faith told me to stick out my tongue. He wanted to anoint it with oil. Our church didn't use the typical virgin olive oil. Instead, we had oil containing frankincense and myrrh. It smelled great, but, as I was about to discover, it tasted horrible.

To me, it seemed like a very strange thing to do, but Pastor Fjordbak was insisting that my tongue had to be anointed too, so I obediently stuck it out, and he proceeded to pour the ghastly mixture onto my tongue (and I don't mean "a little dab will do ya").

Then he poured what remained in the bottle over my head. I looked like a drowned rat, but the power of God was so thick and heavy on me I couldn't stand up under it, and I buckled to the floor like a sack of potatoes.

Next, Brother Fjordbak motioned for two men on the front row to come and pick me up and he instructed them to carry me around to the people in the congregation who needed healing. They stood me up and held me in place and then let my hand plop onto the people who wanted prayer. It happened without any help from me, and yet the result was that those folks I prayed for in this very unorthodox way were instantly healed.

Oh, what a powerful time of ministry and healing that was! And yet I was still sick and in pain. Crohn's disease was working overtime in my body. As bizarre as it sounds, as long as I was under the anointing of God, there was no pain, but as soon as I had finished praying for people, sickness and pain again wracked my body.

During another evening service, I was leading worship when Jonna made an emergency call to the church. She had stayed home that night because Trey was running a fever. The pastor interrupted the worship, approaching the platform and telling me to hurry home because Trey's fever had reached above 105°. Joanna couldn't get it down, and she thought Trey needed to be taken to the emergency room.

I ran from the platform, hit the doors and was in my car faster than a speeding bullet. On the way home, the Holy Spirit spoke to me very softly and said, "Who is the priest of your house?"

I responded, "Lord, You are."

"No!" He said. "Who is My priest in your house?"

"Lord, I am!" I replied this time.

"Then go in and rebuke the fever as My priest, as My representative in your house."

As I flew into the house, Jonna sat holding Trey, who was very hot and limp. I took him from her and began to pray. Jonna exclaimed, "I've already done that, so we need to go now!"

She was right, but I had to pray in order to be obedient to what I had felt the Lord directing me. I prayed this simple prayer, "Father, as the priest of this home, I command this fever to leave immediately from Trey's body and from my home." I kissed him and handed him back to Jonna, and when she took him, he was completely cool to the touch.

Trey opened his eyes, looked Jonna square in the face, and said, "Momma, I'm hungry." (He has been repeating that phrase ever since).

Later, Jonna and I discussed what happened in the room that day. She had prayed for Trey and God had not healed him, yet when I prayed, God did the healing. I think He was teaching me priestly authority, regardless of how I felt in my own body. We have authority, regardless of our circumstances or conditions. As believers, God gives us authority to walk in, no matter how we may feel.

On July 1st of that year, Jonna and I welcomed our second son, Corey Edward. What a cool kid! He is so witty and such a blessing to us, just like his brother Trey. To be honest, I didn't even remember Corey being born because I was again severely ill. The disease had taken a major turn for the worse, and I was rushed to the emergency room on July 4th.

The emergency room doctor, Dr. Bone, quickly determined that I was in real trouble and in need of emergency surgery. He told Joanna, "Donald has developed such a high tolerance for pain that he has endured the pain so long that the disease is about to kill him." I had gone through this so many times that I had now let it get out of hand. The Crohn's disease had caused a fistula, a pocket of infection, in the wall of my stomach that would have to be cut out, and then the resulting hole would have to heal from the inside out. So, instead of being home enjoying my new son, I was in the hospital having six feet of intestines removed and a hole left in my side as large as my fist where the fistula had been cut out. I didn't remember much after the first shot of Demerol.

My parents arrived in Dallas while I was in surgery, and when I awakened, I remember so vividly hearing my dad praying for me, "Jesus, God, if You will heal my boy, I will serve You." I've never believed in making deals with God, but I was lying there praying, "God, if this is what it takes to see my Daddy serve You, I would endure it over and over again." Today my dad is the biggest testifier of God's healing and grace of anyone I know. I believe that night God did good things in both of us.

When I became fully conscious, all I could do was tell my dad what a wonderful young lady I had married and how much I loved her. At times, she had faith when I had none, hope when mine was gone, and strength when I was weak.

Following the surgery, my recovery did not go well, and I soon found myself in pain once again. But now, something in me changed: I embraced being sick. There comes a time in your spirit that you have to lay hold of a tenacity, a hope in you that says, "It doesn't matter what I see, and it doesn't matter what everybody else says. I have to believe God because I have heard from Him." I stopped allowing other people to pray for my healing. I didn't even pray for my own healing anymore. I became like Job when he said, *"Though He slay me, yet will I trust Him"* (Job 13:15). I knew God had a greater purpose for me, and I surrendered to that purpose, no matter my personal comfort or status.

Each of us must realize that storms will come and beat against our house of hope. Floodwaters will rise in our lives. The question isn't if the waters and storms will come, but what will be standing after they pass.

Sometimes, when people are in the midst of a storm, they throw hope out. But you can go through the storm without the storm going through you. In the New Living Translation, Proverbs 13:12 says, *"Hope deferred makes the heart sick, but when the desire comes, it is a tree of life."* Have you ever had hope in something and when it repetitively did not come to pass, you just got sick about it? I think we all understand that feeling. Hold on to your hope through every storm.

For some, the storm they are facing is a relationship problem. It could be marriage, for example. For others, it's a job or a promotion. We can all fill in the blanks. I was battling Crohn's disease, a terrible disease that can be in remission one day and then show up in another part of the digestive tract the next.

. . . . . . . . . . . . . . . . . . . . . . . . . . . . . .

## For some, the storm they are facing is a relationship problem. It could be marriage, for example. For others, it's a job or a promotion. We can all fill in the blanks

. . . . . . . . . . . . . . . . . . . . . . . . . . . . . .

One of the things that would cause a flare-up of the disease and put me back in the hospital was stress and the resulting worry. The Bible tells us: *"Be anxious for nothing"* (Philippians 4:6). Jesus taught, *"Which of you by worrying can add one cubit to his stature"* (Matthew 6:27)? The number one cause of death in men today is heart failure brought on by stress. To combat the stress in my life, that could otherwise prove fatal, I began to develop a philosophy, a mindset, that would help me survive. I now had a different expectancy, a desired result. I had a dream God had given to me. My hope would attack whatever the enemy's hope for my life happened to be at the moment. I would hope against hope.

It didn't matter what anybody said or what they thought; my hope would hold firm. My hope now became a three-fold braided cord, for I now accompanied it with faith and love. And my hope was in God, not in me.

I still had a promise from God, and it was going to come to pass, not because I had the ability, but because God in me had the ability. Although I felt bad, I applied my new philosophy and continued to function physically with the help of medications.

In 1994, Jonna and I were invited to go to Sapulpa, Oklahoma, to become part of the church staff under the leadership of Pastor Scott Olson. I loved Pastor Scott and considered him to be one of the most genuine, transparent men of God I knew. He wasn't perfect, but he was real, and in the days to come, I learned many lessons while under his ministry.

Pastor Scott became a mentor to me. He was much more than a pastor, for he taught me in areas other than ministry, such as being a good husband, provider and father, and he modeled all of those through his own struggles and transparency.

I learned during this time that not everyone can deal with a pastor's humanity. People draw on your anointing, but oftentimes they can't handle the fact that, as a minister, you are, first and foremost, a man.

Ministry times in Oklahoma were great, even though it was the most difficult place we had ever served. At the same time, it became the most fruitful for the Kingdom of God.

Sapulpa was in the epicenter of the Faith Movement, and to confess that you had a chronic sickness in that environment would bring a hundred faith-filled people praying for you in a matter of seconds. So I did what every great faith man does: I didn't tell anyone I was sick, except for my pastor and his wife. Remember, I had given up on praying for healing and especially having other people pray for me. I was not bitter or angry, nor full of doubt or unbelief; I was just trusting the Father's promise and His timing.

Sometimes I found trusting to be harder than praying, screaming, anointing and crying. Still, I just waited on the Lord to come through, just as He had spoken. I continued to pray for other people and to see tremendous results, but I was still sick in my own body.

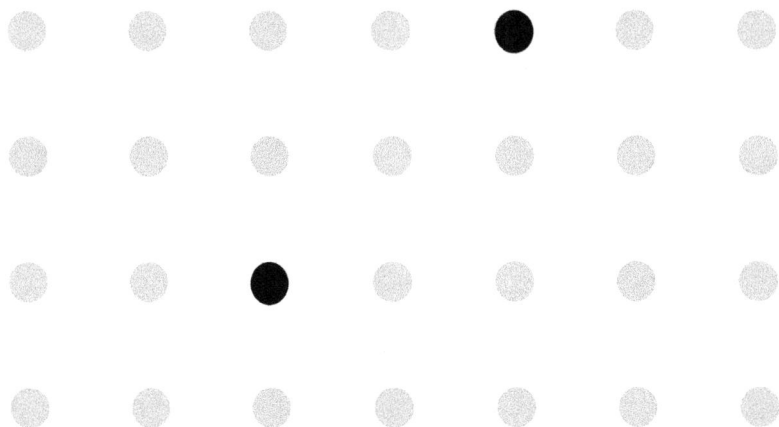

## CHAPTER 6

# "IN DUE SEASON"

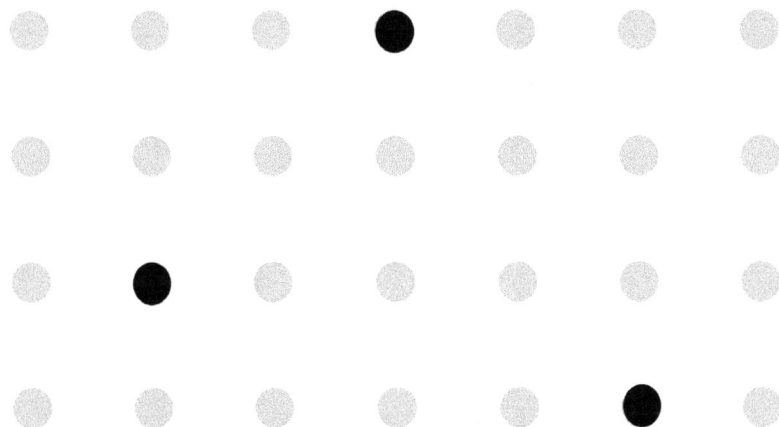

After being in Oklahoma for a couple of years, Jonna and I began to long to return to Texas, and we talked to God about it. But it just didn't seem to be our season, so we had to wait.

One of my favorite biblical heroes has always been David, the humble shepherd boy who became king over all of Israel. There are many things I love about this man, and I could write about them all, but that will have to keep for another book. Here I want to address a couple of pertinent things that have impressed me and encouraged my walk with the Lord.

First and foremost, God said of David, *"I have found David the son of Jesse, a man after my own heart, who will do all My will"* (Acts 13:22). I love that! God didn't say David was perfect; He said he was a man after His own heart. The key is in the word *after,* which means "in pursuit of." The important thing to remember is that this doesn't suggest that David had arrived, but rather that he was "in pursuit of" the heart of God. What a message of hope that is for all of us!

The truth is that David was probably one of the most flawed men in the entire Bible. He was a great giant-killer, and yet he still had some serious personal issues. Part of this was due to the fact that he had come from a rather dysfunctional family. When the prophet came to his father, Jesse's home, Jesse called all of his sons to the party to see who would be anointed to be the new king of Israel, but he failed to invite his son, David. Oh, I am so glad that when others overlook us—even those in our own household—God knows where we are, even if it is in the field taking care of the sheep.

That day, in spite of Jesse's failure, David was anointed to be king of Israel, but the time to assume that position did not arrive quickly, and it is always a struggle when you know you have been called—"chosen"—and yet opportunity is not presented to you. So what do you do in such circumstances? You must be obedient and faithful where you are and take advantage of the time to work on your "stuff"—your character. David was a man after God's own heart because he was willing to do the will of God. Our obedience is evidence of our hope.

One should never allow an anointing or a position to carry you where your character cannot keep you. Some have allowed their gifts, charm and charisma to take them places and into positions that their character could not keep them, and the result is that they turn out to be an embarrassment to themselves and to others, often to the entire Body of Christ. We need to work on our own "stuff" while we're still on the backside of the mountain and not wait to do it on the stage of ministry or life.

. . . . . . . . . . . . . . . . . . . . . . . . . . . . . . . .

> # One should never allow an anointing or a position to carry you where your character cannot keep you.

. . . . . . . . . . . . . . . . . . . . . . . . . . . . . . . .

David began his rise to prominence after one of his greatest victories, killing the giant Goliath. It may be the most well-known of all Bible stories. The theme of facing the giant is even used today in secular sporting events; we all root for the underdog, the little shepherd boy, the young David.

David left the battlefield that day, dragging the head of the giant all the way to Jerusalem, a twenty-six-mile journey. Get this picture: David probably weighed 150 lbs soaking wet, and it has been estimated that Goliath's head may have weighed as much as 125 lbs, and yet David drug it twenty-six miles to Jerusalem to demonstrate the victory of the Lord for His people.

In record time, David was promoted from the shepherd's fields to the palace of Saul, the current king, and that was not a good idea. Although David had been anointed to be king, it was not yet his season, and we should never enter a position until it is our season. If we do, it might cost us dearly. Over the years, I have served in difficult situations, often under overbearing leaders, but I had to bide my time, realizing that it was not yet my season.

Saul had a nasty spirit, and the spirit of Saul will always be threatened by the spirit of David. Saul was out to keep position, rank and title. He had no desire to invest in or set up the next generation for success. This is how you know you are operating in the spirit of Saul: when the job, ministry, family, business, or church is all about you and not the next generation, then it is the spirit of Saul. The spirit of Saul says goofy things such as:

> *"I had to learn it the hard way, and so will you."*
> *"No one ever helped me, so why should I help you?"*

When you fight more for you than for the next generation and investing in their lives, you are operating in the spirit of Saul.

Still, in spite of Saul's nasty spirit, David needed to serve in the house of Saul. It was in the house of Saul where God worked all of "Saul" out of David. I really believe that if David would not have worked for Saul, he would have been just like Saul.

During his time under Saul, David was threatened, and there were several actual attempts on his life, yet he did not assume the position he was anointed for until Saul was off the scene. It took sixteen years of running from a madman who was trying to kill him, but David survived. He not only survived; God built a house for David.

When I say a "house," I mean the legacy that came forth from the lineage of David, and it happened because David did things God's way, not the way everyone else did. Oh, David was not perfect by any means, and yet God built him a heritage. That is why I, too, have hope.

At one point, those who had become the followers of David encouraged him to kill Saul. They took him to where Saul was, and it would have been very easy for David to take things into his own hands. Instead of killing Saul, David only cut off part of Saul's garment (to prove to the king that he had been there and could have done him harm), and yet afterward, the younger man repented before the Lord for even having done that much toward touching God's anointed.

Later we read in the Scriptures that David had a son who was heir to his throne. This son's name was Absalom. The Bible tells us that the boy was handsome, tall, and had beautiful, long hair. But Absalom didn't do things the way his father, David, had modeled them. Instead, Absalom tried to assume a position and title through manipulation and force.

As you read the story of Absalom and what his end was, you will note that David actually relinquished the throne to his son because relationships were always more important to him than title or position. But Absalom wasn't satisfied with that. He wanted everything his father had.

Joab, a servant of David, got into an altercation with Absalom, and Absalom took off on horseback. As he was riding under a tree, his long hair got so caught in the branches of the tree that it jerked him off of his horse and left him dangling high above the ground. He was helpless, an easy target, and when Joab caught up with him, he cut off his head.

The reason Joab cut off Absalom's head was that the lad had dared to try to overthrow his father and usurp his throne. But there is a greater truth here: the hair and head of Absalom represent headship, government, and authority. He tried to assume headship, government, and authority by force and out of season, and in doing so, he failed to serve his father faithfully. Rather than serve, he rebelled, and it cost him his future, his title, his position, his government, his headship (and his head).

No matter where and with whom you are serving, serve until God promotes you. Never rise up against God's anointed, for you will always pay the price for it. It will only be a matter of time, and someone will rise up against you. If you are working for a Saul, let God work all the Saul out of you. If you find yourself behaving like an Absalom toward those in authority over you, repent. Ask God to forgive you and then serve that leader, boss or whomever it is to the best of your ability, and in due season the Lord will promote you (because you did it the right way).

. . . . . . . . . . . . . . . . . . . . . . . . . . . . . . . . .

## No matter where and with whom you are serving, serve until God promotes you.

. . . . . . . . . . . . . . . . . . . . . . . . . . . . . . . . .

We all have the capacity to be a Saul, a David or an Absalom. I believe our choices, especially in difficult times, will shape us into which one of these we will become.

Now back to 1996: When we prayed about leaving Sapulpa, no doors seemed to open, and my health was deteriorating. I visited a gastroenterologist in the Tulsa area, and he ran a series of tests on me, all the same tests I had been through multiple times before. Thankfully, there had now been much technological advancement, and the tests were not nearly as painful as they had been before. Following these tests, we had a consultation with the doctor, and I will never forget the conversation.

Remember, I was by now numb to Crohn's disease and the bad news I had been given concerning it in the past, so I was not about to panic, no matter what the doctor reported. But now, at the consultation, the doctor claimed that I had the worst case of Crohn's disease he had ever seen.

"Doc," I said, "if you've seen two or three cases, then I'm not that concerned, but if you've seen thousands, that might make me a bit nervous."

His regretful reply was: "Donald, I have seen many, and you have the worst I have ever seen. I suggest you have another section done." (This was the surgery in which they went in and removed a section of my intestinal tract).

The doctor continued, "You may want to go home and think about this, because after the surgery this time you will be left with a colostomy bag."

Then he asked, "What is it you do for a living?"

"I'm a minister," I answered.

He proceeded to inform me that I should consider resigning my position in ministry, as ministry is known to be one of the most stressful jobs in America.

But to me, ministry is not something you choose. God chooses you for ministry, and it's a calling. But how could I explain to that doctor that a person can't just turn off the calling of God? I simply and respectfully replied that leaving the ministry was not an option for me.

His next suggestion was that I go home for the weekend and discuss the situation with Jonna and then return the following Monday for a new series of endoscopy tests and be prepared for surgery. But surgery was no longer an option for me, any more than was quitting the ministry. I honestly didn't give it much thought over the weekend. Jonna and I talked about it once, maybe twice, throughout those days, but I had already definitely decided there would be no more surgery.

Sunday evening, March 6, 1996, was like any other evening for me. Jonna was putting the boys to bed in the next room. Alone on the living room couch, I was catching up on the news and sports headlines for the day and actively participating in my usual habit of channel surfing ESPN to catch the latest basketball scores.

As I was flying through the channels, TBN briefly appeared, and the Holy Spirit whispered to my spirit and said, "STOP!" Finally recognizing the voice of God, after I had gone through the next three channels, I went back to TBN. Obedience is key, even in the small things.

Now the Holy Spirit spoke to me again. That still, small voice on the inside of my spirit prompted me to call in and give my prayer request. As I picked up the phone and began to dial, the guest singer was performing "I Pledge Allegiance to the Lamb."

On my first call, I got a busy signal and, frankly, I am glad I did because the prayer request I was going to give would not have been the correct one. The request I had in mind was to have someone pray with me for doors to open to leave Oklahoma and return to Texas, but the Father had something else for me, something I had not personally prayed for in more than four years.

The Holy Spirit spoke again to me and said, "My servant will be back on the screen, and the word he has is for you." I didn't even know who the guest speaker was that evening, but I did know God's voice, and His presence was all over me, so much so that all I could do now was weep.

When the guest speaker returned following the song, it was Dr. Oral Roberts. I vividly remember his huge hands being lifted up and him saying, "Tonight there is a young man watching this program. At times your abdomen hurts so severely you have fallen down in the fetal position in stores, malls, and many other public places, just trying to get some relief from the pain. Tonight God is healing you!"

Immediately, I was engulfed in heat. The Holy Spirit spoke to me again, and it was so clear—not audible, but just as clear as if it had been. The Lord said to me, "Every tear ever shed, I heard it and saw it, but this was the night I set aside to heal you." I jumped to my feet and ran into the bedroom, calling to Jonna and pulling her into the living room, so that I could tell her what was happening to me.

I was burning up, completely swallowed up by heat to the point of sweating, and I don't normally sweat. Jonna kept trying to see if I had a fever, but she found my body cool to the touch. I told her that God was healing me.

Dr. Roberts was preparing to close the program with prayer when he instructed, "Reach out your hands toward this screen and let's agree in faith." A basket of emotions, I knelt beside my beautiful wife, and together we reached upward toward the television screen in an act of faith, and we cried, prayed and believed God together.

As Brother Roberts began to pray, the heat rushed out of my head down to my mid-section. At the same time, the heat rushed up from my feet and legs to the same area. Heat concentrated in my abdominal region, while Dr. Roberts prayed, and I didn't know whether to ask God to stop or continue. It was so hot that it was almost painful, yet it felt so good I wanted it to continue forever.

When Dr. Roberts finished praying, the heat dispersed back through my entire body. For an hour and forty minutes afterward, everywhere I went in our home heat continued to overpower me, but now it was like a wonderful feeling that I embraced. It's difficult to explain. The things of God are often hard to explain, especially His signs and wonders. They wouldn't be wonders if they didn't make us wonder at times.

When I could catch my breath, the first thing I wanted to do was call my mother to share with her what had just taken place. Jonna cautioned that my parents would already be asleep, but I knew I had to let them know the good news. As I told my mom what had happened, she wept, and she had my dad get on another phone so he could hear too. I told them everything, from the bad news the doctor had just given us, to the wonderful healing encounter with Jesus that had followed.

I had one more thing to do, and that was to keep the doctor's appointments on the following day. That next day, Monday morning, I be-bopped into the hospital prepared to take another set of endoscopies. As the doctor inquired how I was feeling, I proudly pronounced, "I feel great, Doc! No pain!"

Surprised, he questioned, "None?"

He proceeded to explain the upcoming test procedures, but honestly, I didn't hear much of anything he was saying. I was so excited about what they were *not* going to find. In a matter of seconds, I drifted into "la-la land" with an IV in my arm and Jonna went to the waiting area. Later she related to me what happened while I was asleep.

After a while, the doctor had come to the waiting room and asked Jonna for her permission to run the test again because they had "found some things which did not seem quite right." Her response was that if I was still under sedation, then they should do whatever it took. She was not being uncaring, but she was as weary with the disease as I was. And we were both ready for some relief from it.

When the second procedure was complete and I was awake again, we were instructed to come back to the doctor's office at 4:30 that afternoon. In my heart, I knew there was nothing to be found, and I kept telling Jonna that the doctor only wanted to meet to inform us that the Crohn's disease was gone. She tried to caution me, not wanting me to get my hopes up and then be disappointed again, but I was as sure of my healing as I had ever been of anything in my life.

The appointed time didn't arrive any too soon for me, for I was so looking forward to it. I walked into the doctor's office looking like the kid who had taken the last piece of candy out of the candy jar. Full of faith, I was anxious to hear his report.

Jonna and I were directed to a very professional-looking consultation room, with fine prints on the walls and lovely cherry furniture. Unlike a patient's room, this was especially nice. It was where patients are taken to be given "options." We were told to make ourselves comfortable and the doctor would arrive shortly.

Soon, Dr. Fucci entered the room like a man on a mission. We began with small talk. He asked how I was feeling, and my response that I was feeling "Great!" He continued with the small talk, as he retrieved some colored photographs and placed them on a viewing board. On a more serious tone, he continued, "Donald, this picture is your intestinal tract the last time we did endoscopies."

Next, he placed another picture on the viewing board and asked, "Do you know what this is?"

I answered, "No sir, I don't, but it looks like someone's intestinal tract."

I was correct: it was someone's. The picture on the left was my intestinal tract from the previous week and in it I could plainly see all the ulcers and discoloration caused by the Crohn's disease. The picture on the right of the viewing board was "someone's" intestinal tract and this one appeared to be normal and healthy.

At this point, I was getting nervous as to why he wanted to show me someone else's healthy intestines. He marveled as he reported, "Donald, the issue is that the picture on the right is a picture of your intestinal tract from this morning's tests."

With that, I smiled so big it was comical. He looked to me for any explanation of what might have made the difference. Ready to reveal the good news, I proceeded to tell him the wonderful story of what happened when Oral Roberts prophesied to me and what I experienced.

With eyes misty from tears, the doctor looked at me and said that he would not have believed it if he had not seen the proof before his eyes. He removed a pen from his lab coat pocket and wrote **MIRACLE** across the top of my medical form. That document forms the basis of the cover for this book and is a repeated graphic element throughout. It tells the story, perhaps better than I can do it with many words.

He removed a pen from his lab coat pocket and wrote **MIRACLE** across the top of my medical form.

The doctor's final instructions to me that day were to return to see him if and when I ever had any similar problems, and my last words to him were to confirm my strong convictions: "Doc," I said, "I will never see you again this side of Heaven, at least not for *this* problem." I was just that sure of what God had done.

Leaving the doctor's office for the last time that day, we picked up our boys from the babysitter and went home to celebrate. And we have been celebrating now for more than sixteen years, completely healed! During those years, I have never needed any medications, doctor's visits or had any upset stomach due to Crohn's disease. Some Crohn's sufferers have experienced long periods of remission, but only with the aid of regular medications. I haven't needed even one single pill. That night, March 6th 1996, God completely healed me, and I give Him thanks every day verbally and by the way I try to live.

Many years after I was healed, I had the opportunity to share my miracle with Dr. Roberts through a letter. In his response, he wrote, "Donald, I am 89 years old now and in the sunset of this life, but I am committed to finishing my course. I send to you a blessing of the 'Old Prophet' for the further enrichment of your life in Christ and the success of all you undertake in His name." I have included the full letter in the book on pages 23-24. I hope you are as encouraged by it as I have been.

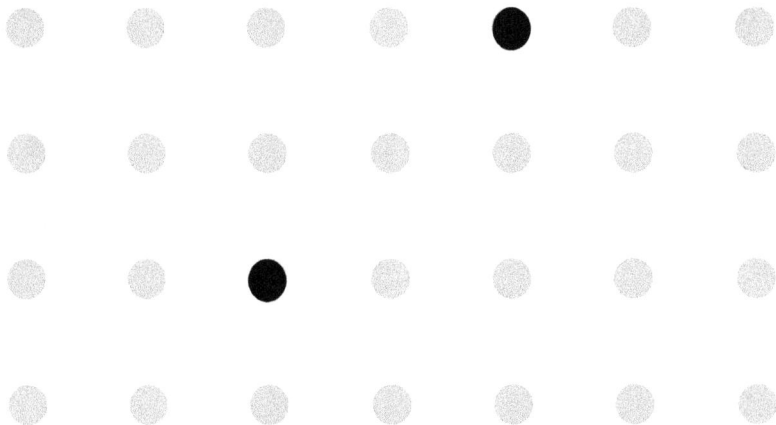

# CHAPTER 7

# FAITH, HOPE, AND LOVE

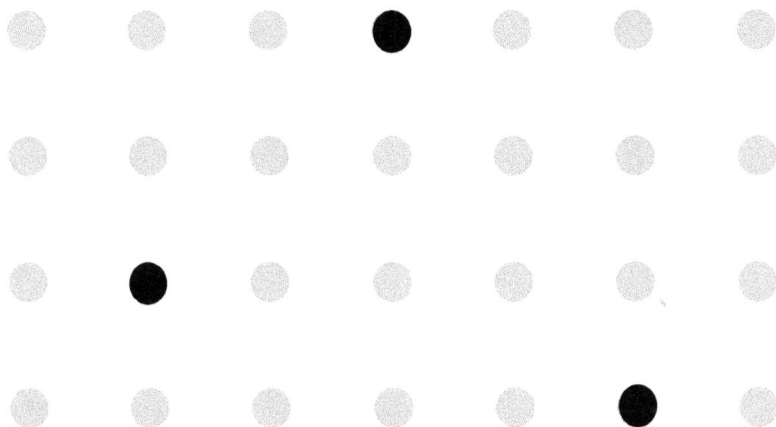

M y healing, as is the case with many miracles, goes beyond me. It became Jonna's miracle and inspiration too, and from it, she learned so much that moved her faith forward to a place of greater hope and greater love. The following is her account of our miracle:

*I hear the loud shrieking, and it makes my hair stand on end, as the large family leaves the messy trauma room. As I warily approach the group, a short Hispanic lady jumps out and grabs my arm tightly. With a scary desperation in her eyes and her tiny body shaking, she screams out the word, "Why? Why? Why?" Over and over I hear it repeated, as she now uses her other fisted hand to softly hit my chest. Waves of emotion come and go, and I find myself being pulled to the floor beside her.*

*She lies there in a heap, as stretchers and hospital staff busily pass by, for she refuses to leave the area where her son took his last breath, and she won't let go of me, the nurse who heard her son's last words.*

*Thankfully I cannot relate to this woman's loss of a son, but I can relate to her desperate cries of "Why?" I asked myself that same question plenty of times over the years.*

*The definition of the word why is "for what purpose, reason, cause or intention." Here was a man who loved God and wanted to be a minister for life, to help people and trumpet the cause of Christ, and he developed some random sickness that no one in his family line had ever had, and no one knew how to cure. It wasn't fair! Who in their right mind wouldn't ask why? Who wouldn't wonder if what was happening was a test or a sign?*

*For many years people would ask me why I thought Don was sick. Did I do something wrong? Did he do something that he needed to repent of? Did we not have enough faith? Unfortunately, many well-meaning people gave us advice, and most of it left me feeling even worse. I would overhear someone telling him that if he would just change his diet he would be healed, if he would follow certain healing evangelists around the country, his healing would come, or if he changed his stressful occupation (which happened to be that of a youth pastor) that the miracle would come. My favorite one was that he should repent of all the sin in his life in public, and surely then he would be made whole. After all is said and done, people do mean well, but believe it or not, we tried it ALL, and nothing worked.*

*I wish I could say that I have always been the wife full of faith and power, but the truth is that I wasn't. I was sometimes very fearful and vacillated between faith and fear. Afraid of the future and of the unknown, I was scared of what was going to happen to me and the kids if something happened to Don. I* would cry at night, without anyone knowing, and it was the result of pure helplessness. I felt there was nothing I could say or do to help my husband.

There was more: Along the way, one of the doctors told me that statistics showed that Crohn's disease might well be hereditary in males and that I should keep a close watch on both of my boys for any signs or symptoms. This, of course, gave me yet something else to heap upon my already hefty plate of worry.

From then on, every tummy ache or childhood sickness my boys suffered would cause a tight knot to form in my stomach, and my mind would go wild with thoughts. I was a disaster. I tried, through it all, to keep a "happy" face, when in reality, my heart was very heavy.

It's easy to forget that we are the King's kids, and we have a Father who has never-ending resources. His promise, "For I know the thoughts that I think toward you, says the Lord, thoughts of peace and not evil, to give you a future and a hope" (Jeremiah 29:11) is more than enough for us, so why do we find ourselves in crippling unbelief? Even encouraging scriptures such as this can seem hollow and very far away when someone we love is going through hard times.

In fact, there is a mentality that starts to develop in you, and no matter what people may say to encourage you, you will *not or cannot receive it. I personally suffered from this mentality and realized many years later that I was operating as a victim.*

*Even though it wasn't me who was sick and in piercing pain, I started to think that it was somehow all about me:*

*I deserve better.*
*What am I going to do?*
*I can't seem to help this situation*
*I want a normal family.*
*I am tired of this.*
*I....*

*It was endless. In the process, I forgot about the person who was suffering and, at times, I actually felt like I was suffering more than he, and that was a lot.*

*Don would severely hurt at times, so badly that he would fall to the floor and get into a curled up or fetal position and cry, and it happened sometimes in public places. The first time I experienced this first-hand was while we were still dating. I looked up from Don's side, where he was lying on the floor, and felt a whole mix of emotions.*

*I couldn't help but see the stares from the people at the mall. A few curiously approached and asked if we needed help or if they should call 911, and others hurried by, looking scared and not wanting to get involved. I never once remember wondering why I was dating this guy who had this disease that seemed so debilitating. I really didn't care that I looked strange, as I lay over Don in front of the food court by JC Penney's, because no one understood what this guy on the floor was going through.*

*What was so amazing to see was how people stayed far away from something they didn't understand so that they did not have to deal with it. Sometimes it is easier to ignore something in the hope that it might go away. But this evil disease wasn't going anywhere.*

*Not much was known about Crohn's disease back then, so only a few specialists in Houston knew how to deal with it. The only things I truly knew about it were: (1) It caused terrible pain, and (2) There was no known cure.*

*In the first year Don and I were married, he had a few flare-ups, and I would try to block it out of my mind. I knew he had Crohn's disease, but if I tried not to think about it, then it would be like we were a normal couple, and maybe it would just go away.*

*This "normal couple" thought didn't last long, as in 1990 Don had some very bad bouts of the disease and had to be hospitalized several times. I remember the day he was to be discharged from the small hospital near Pleasanton, Texas. He was very hungry, so, being a good wife, I went to the vending machine and got him a snack. Don took two bites of it and started having severe pain again and ended up having to spend two more days in the hospital.*

*Brilliant me had given him popcorn, which is the worst thing he could have eaten. Any seeds or anything rough was forbidden and would literally scrape the intestinal wall because a flare-up is actually swelling, which closes up the tract so that nothing can get through. Even a sip of water moving through can be excruciating. Needless to say, we had to be better educated about what he should eat and not eat.*

*My heart was wishing this disease would just disappear, but I knew this was going to be a struggle of some sort and a challenge to my faith level. I started praying for Don's healing and looking up scriptural confirmation of God's will to heal. In the process, my faith increased dramatically each time God would give me any tiny piece of revelation on the subject.*

*God told Don to start praying specifically for other sick people, so he was quick to lay hands on anyone he heard was suffering any illness. And the law of sowing and reaping is powerful, so we were blessed in amazing ways, just not in the healing department.*

*People would just walk up to us and give us money and gifts, and I was so very grateful. But the desire of my heart was the gift of healing. It was sad to see Don get so skinny, see all his bones in his body, and see him have to wear many layers of clothing so that no one would notice his weight loss. He had* no energy and no appetite, and when he tried to eat, he would get sick and throw up.

It was amazing to see how Don could get through a service, singing, smiling and praying for other people, and often no one even realized what was truly going on in his own life.

Looking back, it amazes me to think how God always provided. The jobs I managed to get (with no previous experience) paid well and always provided insurance. People were amazed at the favor Don had on his life way back then, even in the midst of great suffering. We encountered no financial debt, even with the hundreds of thousands of dollars in hospital, doctor's or surgeon's bills.

## Looking back, it amazes me to think how God always provided.

We were also blessed with amazing pastors with whom we worked, for they loved us and never counted sick days. They worked with Don like none other would have done. While working at North Mesquite Assembly, with Pastor Sipes, for example, Don had to take months off, but we never heard a negative word from those precious people about it. The church brought us food, sent us cards almost daily, babysat two little kids while we went to appointments, and even paid our salary *the whole time. We appreciated it, but like the children of Israel, even in the most wonderful times of blessing, I would lose heart when Don suffered any relapse.*

*I prayed more, attended all the scheduled services, dressed my best, was always on time (and anyone who knows me knows that is a "biggie" for me), taught multiple classes at church, had the biggest smile and the largest Bible, and all so that Don could get healed.*

*One day someone told me to make sure that I never confessed the fact that my husband was sick so that the enemy wouldn't get an advantage over us. So when people would ask about him, I would put my "faith cap" on and lie about how wonderful he was doing. It makes me laugh now, just thinking about it. I was living in a guilt-ridden state, full of condemnation.*

*I truly began to believe that the reason Don was sick was directly related to me. I found myself exhausted from dragging him to every visiting minister in anticipation that my faithfulness, their anointing, and the imported vial of their "special oil" would be the winning combination. On the way home, I would ask if he was feeling better, and he would wearily say, "A little." I would try to muster up a comment that had some excitement to it, but in the back of my mind, I knew things weren't changing for him.*

*Thinking back on it now, the poor guy was probably totally stressed out just from me trying to make things happen. Desperation will make you do things you have never done before. Whether it sounds crazy or not, it is only human to try to take matters into your own hands. That is when we start looking all around and literally grabbing anything or anyone that possibly may offer a glimmer of hope. I was so determined that I hadn't realized I had lost all my faith in WHO God was. I was so wrapped up in my works that I never realized I was relying on my knowledge of God and believed that healing would come with what I was doing.*

*This revelation came to my heart the day the doctor told Don that his Crohn's was back and was the worst case he had ever seen. The surrender started that day, as my spirit took over my exhausted body, and I prayed in the Spirit. I felt like a limp dishrag and didn't want to move, but there were people interceding on my behalf.*

*I didn't know what to pray or how to pray. I literally found myself driving around the "Praying Hands" sculpture at Oral Roberts University that day, and in my heart and mind placing Don's body and our future there in those great bronze palms. I had no other idea or thought about what to do, no other healthy dish, blended juice or pill to have him try. For the first time in our marriage, I gave Don and his sickness to God.*

*You might be wondering: "You were a youth pastor's wife and speaking to kids, imparting wisdom, yet you couldn't believe for yourself?" YES, I just wasn't real about my thoughts and feelings, for fear of judgment by others. Little did I realize that even though I felt alone, I was far from it, because God had so many people praying for us.*

*As soon as I got my focus off of myself and looked upward, I was able to grasp the peace, strength and joy that had always been there, but I had never taken advantage of. The enemy loves to make us think that we are the only ones going through something, so that we will become bitter and depressed and feel rejected. God gave us our church family, friends and physical family, to love us and to help and support us during difficult times.*

*How crazy is the thought that we are surrounded by throngs of people but feel so alone? I think it is just deception from the enemy. Alienation and alignment are opposites of each other. Alienation is isolation and hiding due to thoughts that no one understands or that no one cares, and it can lead you to a place of apathy and despondency. Alignment, on the other hand, is being in a position of agreement or alliance with others in believing or toward a purpose that can bring great hope and life. When you are in a situation that is tragic or things have you in a tail-spin, be aware and be prepared for feelings of isolation. Those are the times when you need other people the most. No matter what they say or do to help, or not help, you need to have a mind and heart of alignment, especially with God's heart, so what you do and think is purposeful and not reactionary.*

*There are so many declarations and promises in God's Word that helped me get through all of this. If you are feeling alone and in a mess, claim your promise by using the declarations listed in the book in Appendix A.*

*After this awareness came, I began to live by the philosophy: "I don't know WHY, but what I DO know is that God is faithful." I have used that sentence now for years to explain many questions and many things that we will never understand and truly do not need to comprehend on this side of Heaven. Over our house and family, I began to claim Jeremiah 29:11–14, Proverbs 3:5–6, Mark 11:22–24 and many other promises that are not specifically focused on healing.*

*It's crazy when you wake up one day and realize that every prayer I had been praying and much of the energy I was expending in life was just for one area. There was not a healthy balance. I was living on only one "food group" and never knew it.*

*In this light, "You are what you eat" comes to mean something totally different. When all that is set in front of you is a situation, and everything you do is filtered through that situation, then you are living very unbalanced. We were not created to carry such heavy weights.*

*After Don's surgery, he began to develop hernias when he tried to lift anything heavy, and he had to get a wire mesh implant to reinforce the walls of his abdomen. Then he was placed on a slow exercise regimen which ensured that his back muscles and abdominal muscles would compliment and support each other.*

*Finally, after months, he was able to again lift things without fear of re-injuring himself. God wants to do the heavy work for us. All He asks for is faith in Who He is and in His timing.*

*The night that Don called out to me to come and check his temperature, I thought it was just a regular evening of him not feeling well. And, trust me, I had started developing a resentment of his sickness. I mean: I get sick too, but no one ever takes care of me. Self-pity, as well as selfishness, was developing, and I didn't like the feeling. It was like an infection, and I was well aware of it.*

*I remember asking God to give me strength. After all, I was the mom of two very rambunctious boys, and I also worked a full-time job, as well as being the youth pastor's wife, and I was becoming overwhelmed by it all.*

*I had just gotten five-year-old Trey and three-year-old Corey asleep that night (and that was a job in itself). I had almost fallen asleep myself when Don called me, and I sleepily walked into a living room that was filled with only the light from the television. But I instantly felt the mighty presence of God.*

*I believe every hair on my body stood on end as Don told me calmly that he was "burning up." I quickly touched his forehead, and it was cold to the touch, but he insisted that he was burning up. He had a child-like look of peacefulness on his face, and he wasn't complaining of any pain or nausea. He told me that he felt a strange sensation that was focused on his stomach, and he started rambling on about a TV program and Oral Roberts and calling in to their prayer line.*

*What was different about this moment was that God told me, "I'm doing what I promised." I wasn't absolutely sure what that meant, but whatever God promised, I was ready to receive it. I remember sitting on the floor next to Don and praying quietly while he wept. I was assured that God was killing off something and forming something new in his body. I asked God to forgive me at that moment for my selfishness and for my unbelief, and then peace came over me like a flood. Don went to bed that night and slept with no pain for the first time in a very long while.*

*The next week was a whirlwind of excitement, as Don's tests came out negative for everything that had been positive before. Anemia was gone in his blood tests, and no ulcers were seen in his colonoscopy, even after a repeat exam! We were all in shock. Faith rose up in us so great that we were looking for people to pray for.*

*Today I am a nurse at one of the largest trauma centers in the country, and I have the opportunity to treat people in crisis every day. I want to be that shoulder that someone needs to cry on. I want to be that voice of hope in the face of amazing obstacles.*

*The short paragraph at the beginning of this chapter is a true story of a woman who was clinging to me in her darkest hour. People need to know we care, and we need to take the time out of our busy lives to offer them compassion and love, no matter how uncomfortable it is for us. It is what Jesus would do.*

*I don't like grief and sad news, but I am not going to run from it, because I have something to offer. It doesn't have anything to do with ME, but it has ALL to do with HIM. I may not be the person with all the answers, but I have some great resources to offer. I know a God who is faithful, and no matter what you might be going through right now or what you might have encountered in your past, He is the only answer you need.*

Jonna Gibson

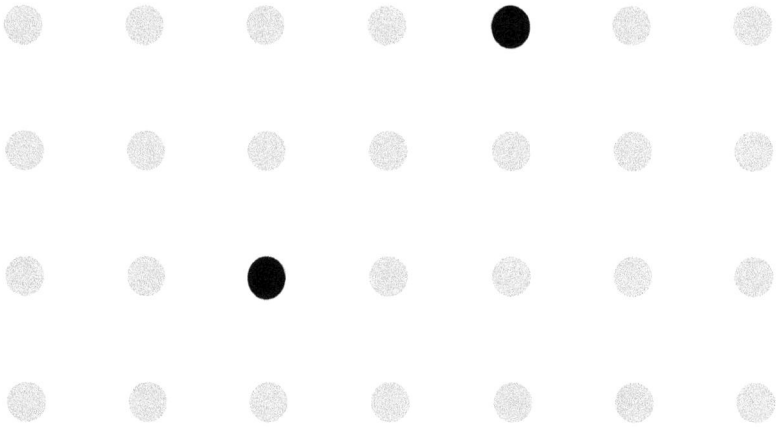

## CHAPTER 8

# HOPE THROUGH YOUR PROCESS

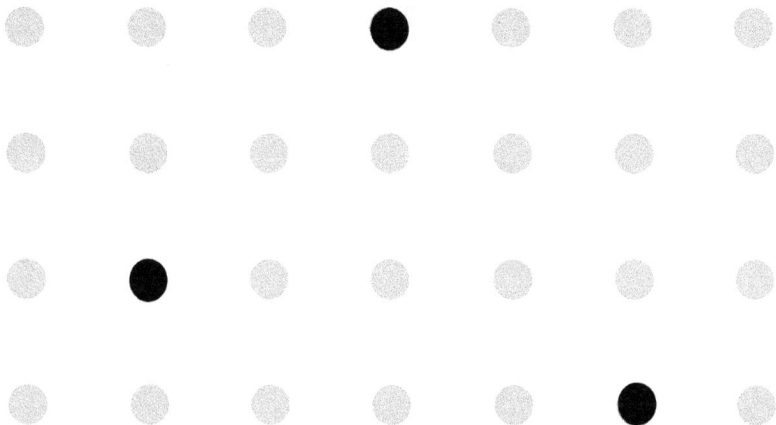

There are several other thoughts I feel compelled to express before closing this book:

## ON THE CONTINUING IMPACT OF MY MIRACLE

God didn't intend my miracle to be limited to what it did for me. I'm grateful for the miracle, but I see how Jonna's life has been strengthened in the process, and I see how our kids' lives have been impacted as well. I would also like to think that people are still being impacted in my congregation and my community through the testimony of this miracle and by how I now live my life because of it. And I trust that my process will continue to impact the lives of others, as God continues to give me inspiration and an anointing that will reach out to those in need.

. . . . . . . . . . . . . . . . . . . . . . . . . . . . . . . . .

### God didn't intend my miracle to be limited to what it did for me.

. . . . . . . . . . . . . . . . . . . . . . . . . . . . . . . . .

## ON NEVER TAKING GOD FOR GRANTED

God is so gracious and good to us that often we take it for granted. For example, when we moved to Pleasanton, the job that was available for Jonna provided immediate insurance coverage and paid in full for Trey's birth. That was a miracle, and the fact that she was pregnant prior to getting the job and was still covered was an even greater miracle. That just doesn't happen in the society we live in today, and yet the same insurance company also covered all of my pre-existing issues.

When we moved to Dallas, the same situation occurred, this time with a different insurance company. Corey's birth was covered, along with all my surgery and medication expenses for treating the Crohn's disease.

Upon arrival in Sapulpa, Jonna went to work for a large, regional insurance office in Tulsa and, once again, her insurance coverage went into effect immediately, and I was completely covered, along with both of our children. Isn't God great!

When we take the favor of God for granted, as happens far too often, or we fail to recognize when He is favoring us, I think the problem is to be found in our focus, especially when we are struggling with a chronic issue, like a sickness. We tend to focus solely on the sickness, the problem or the issue instead of on the areas in which God is visibly at work in our lives. As a result, we fail to see and appreciate all that He is doing.

As noted in an earlier chapter, when John the Baptist was imprisoned, even he failed to see all that Jesus was doing around him, no doubt because of his difficult circumstances. I have learned over the years to look for God at work in all areas and not just focus on one aspect of life.

## ON RECOGNIZING OUR DIVINE PURPOSE IN LIFE

Everything that happens to us in life has a purpose because we are each born with a great destiny in God. Believe it. Genesis declares that you and I were "*formed*" (Genesis 2:7), not spoken into existence like the rest of creation. God stopped speaking for a moment so He could mold and then begin to fashion us as His special creatures. That, among many other things, separates us from the rest of creation. God also created us in His image, and that, too, sets us apart.

This word *formed* in the Hebrew means "to be molded in God's hands as a potter for great purpose." The potter does not put clay on the wheel without first having a thought in mind of what it can become in his hands. In the same way, God already knew you before you were ever formed or knitted in your mother's womb, because He made you. You were not an accident.

If these truths ever get down into your spirit, they will cause your faith and your hope to leap up inside of you. It doesn't matter what anybody says about you; you were created by God, formed by God, on purpose and for a definite purpose. You are a divine design. This is all a result of His great love.

. . . . . . . . . . . . . . . . . . . . . . . . . . . . . . . .

Everything that happens to us in life
has a purpose because we are each
born with a great destiny in God.

. . . . . . . . . . . . . . . . . . . . . . . . . . . . . . . .

## ON BEING IN GOD'S LOVE

*"God is love,"* (1 John 4:8), and we are *"hidden with Christ,"* and Christ is *"in God"* (Colossians 3:3). Therefore, if we are placed in Christ, we are placed in His love, for again, He *is* love. God places us in hope, He places us in Christ, He places us in the Body and, finally, He places us in love. Let us flourish in God's love.

## ON BLOOMING WHERE YOU ARE PLANTED

Each of us must learn how to live and flourish where God has planted us. Adam didn't know how to live in the garden, and he never did learn how, even though God had prepared this very special place for him. Instead, Adam went searching for other things, when he had no reason to be searching for anything at all. Everything he needed had been provided to him right there in the garden. You and I, too, must learn to live in the provision of the place that God has planted us.

It's also important for you to know you are in the right place. When you are in the right place and you know it, your hope will abound, and your joy will be full.

## ON AVOIDING DISAPPOINTMENT THROUGH HOPE

Another wonderful scripture related to the subject of hope says this:

> *Now hope does not disappoint, because the love of God has been poured out in our hearts by the Holy Spirit who was given to us.*
> Romans 5:5

Your journey in life need never be a disappointment, but in order to achieve the desired end, it must be a process of renewing your mind to know and understand God's ways and the journey He has put you on. Every day, as you get into the Word of God and the Word of God gets into you, your mind can be renewed more and more, bringing you ever closer to His perfect plan for your life.

## ON HOPE AND SALVATION AND THE VERY NATURE OF HOPE

In His Word, God also says that we were *"saved in . . . hope"* and goes on to tell us something very important about the very nature of hope:

> *For we were saved in this hope, but hope that is seen is not hope; for why does one still hope for what he sees?*
> Romans 8:24

We don't have to hope for what we already see. It is when we have hope for something as yet unseen and we eagerly wait for it with perseverance and with patience that God honors our hope.

## ON REVIVING HOPE IN DRY TIMES AND WHAT IT MEANS TO BE A PRISONER OF HOPE

If you've ever found yourself in a dry time spiritually, it seems like you are in a pit and that God is a million miles away. But all you need in that moment is one word from Him, one drop of water in your waterless pit, and you'll be able to crawl out of that pit and out of your trouble.

Zechariah declared:

> *Return to the stronghold, you prisoners of hope. Even today I declare that I will restore double to you.*
> Zechariah 9:12–13

You and I are prisoners of hope, held in divine expectation. But being a prisoner of hope does not mean you are in prison. As we have seen, the Scriptures tell us that *"hope deferred makes the heart sick"* (Proverbs 1312). This happens when the deferred desires of hope make us *feel* as if we are in a prison. If, in those moments, we focus only on our desires and not on God's will, then we do become stuck in a prison of frustration. If we are in the pit, and we lose hope, we find ourselves chained to a lot of things—bitterness, worry, anxiety, circumstance, doubt, unbelief and this is frustrating, to say the least.

Frustration is anger over present limitations. Bitterness is anger over past disappointments. Anxiety is anger over future uncertainties. And none of them are good. If we are not careful, these things can literally make us sick.

So, how can we be chained to hope in a good way? We can be chained to hope because we have the Word of God to stand on and we understand that we are in a process and that God has His perfect time for all things. We cannot afford to let the enemy of our soul cause us to become *"weary in well doing"* (Galatians 6:9 and 2 Thessalonians 3:13, KJV) and, thus, to steal our hope and faith in the promises of our heavenly Father.

Divine hope always holds on to the possibility of believing God for the impossible, and that impossibility usually comes when you are at your wit's end. It is in that moment that your difficult situation becomes, for you, not a waterless prison but a veritable well of life.

## ON THE REQUIRED SHAKING

When God spoke from Mount Sinai his voice shook the earth, but now he makes another promise: "Once again I will shake not only the earth but the heavens also." This means that all of creation will be shaken and removed, so that only unshakable things will remain. Since we are receiving a Kingdom that is unshakable, let us be thankful and please God by worshiping him with holy fear and awe. For our God is a devouring fire.

*Keep on loving each other as brothers and sisters.*
Hebrews 12:26–13:31, NLT

Everything in our lives must go through a time of shaking, a time of refining and testing, but through it all, we can be of good cheer because after the shaking takes place, those things that are of God's Kingdom will remain. Therefore stand firm in hope and see God work on your behalf, bringing you forth *"as gold"* (Job 23:10).

It's amazing to me that this scripture passage flows from the *shaking* in verse 28 to the subject of brotherly love in verse 1 of the following chapter. Why is that? I believe the reason for it is that once the shaking has ended, faith, hope and love is what will remain.

## ON THE ETERNAL NATURE OF HOPE

Several times, throughout the book, I have said that God must be our hope. Any other hope will be frustrated here in this life, and only this hope is eternal:

*If we who are [abiding] in Christ have hope only in this life and that is all, then we are of all people most miserable and to be pitied.*
1 Corinthians 15:19, AMP

If all your hopes are wrapped up in this world, you will be a miserable person indeed. I am so glad I have a hope in Christ, that my faith and hope have a future, and that through them, eternity is someday mine.

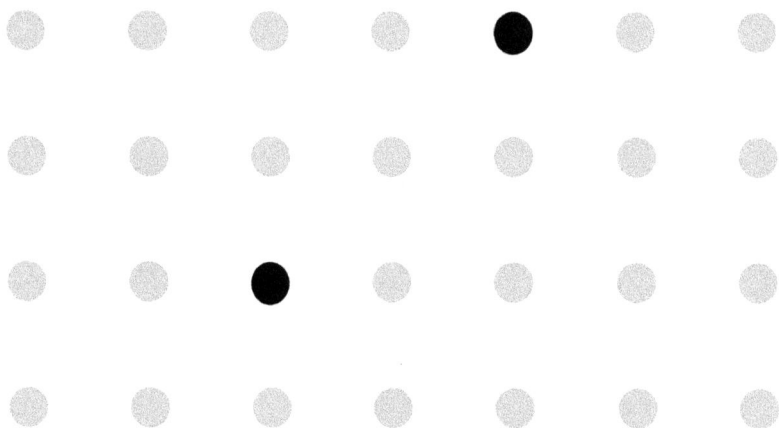

# EPILOGUE

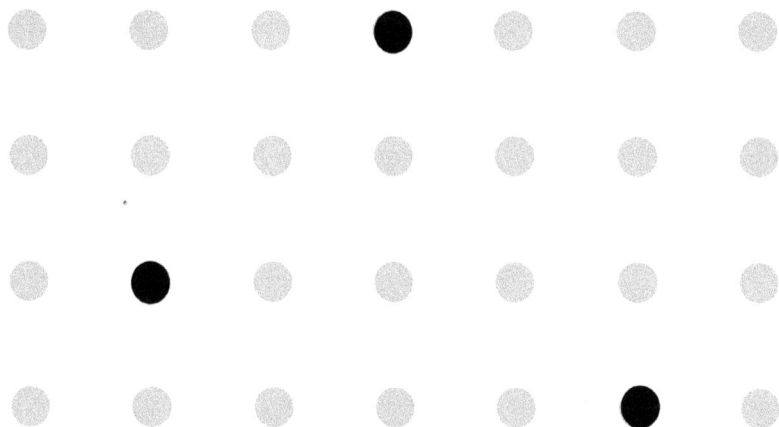

So, it comes down to this: I have written this book for one purpose and one purpose only, and that is for you to be encouraged to have hope through your process, hope in God.

You may have been ill for an extended period of time like I was, but trust me: God has not forgotten you nor lost your address. I don't have all the answers and, honestly, I'm not sure anyone on this planet does. I do know the Lord Jesus loves us, and we cannot become offended with Him when He doesn't come through when, where, and how we think He should.

Since the time I first became ill until today, I have seen God opening deaf ears and healing chronic, degenerative back problems. I have seen Him bring people out of wheelchairs and watched cancer wither and die in other people's bodies. The greatest thrill of all for me, however, has been to witness God healing numerous people of Crohn's and other intestinal diseases. And, of course, He did it for me too.

If you think your circumstances are too big or too bad, then you need to meet my God. He is "able to do exceedingly, abundantly above all that we ask or think" (Ephesians 3:20) or even imagine.

. . . . . . . . . . . . . . . . . . . . . . . . . . . . . . . . . . .

# If you think your circumstances are too big or too bad, then you need to meet my God.

. . . . . . . . . . . . . . . . . . . . . . . . . . . . . . . . . . .

Through the years, I have had opportunity to research healing in God's Word and have found many scriptures and resources to draw from. I've included a listing of scripture verses and accompanying prayers in Appendix B for those who need a guide for healing scriptures. They have helped me through some tough times, and I hope they will help you too.

Hoping through the process starts with realizing you are in a process. God places you in hope, He places you in Christ, and He continually works to transform you into His image and likeness. Your challenge is to keep a balance of faith, hope and love acting as a braided cord to keep you strong through the storms.

My prayer for you today is that God would renew hope in your spirit. To facilitate that hope, I encourage you to write down your expectancies, what you are believing God to do for you. He wants to come through for you and meet your needs, but you need to remain strong in hope. Write it all down.

The prophet Habakkuk wrote, *"Write the vision, . . . make it plain . . . though it tarry, wait for it; because it will surely come"*

(Habakkuk 2:2–3). This word *tarry* is a King James word that means delay or slowness. But *although it seems slow in coming, do*n't give up on your vision or get discouraged with the process. If hope seems to be deferred, cling to your promise ever more firmly. It will surely come.

What is it you are expecting God to do? Don't worry about how He's going to do it. Just say, "God, You have a big problem on Your hands" and then watch Him work.

## A PRAYER FOR SALVATION

If you are in the position I was at seven years of age (and I still find myself there from time to time), you need the Carpenter to come and move into your house (heart). Make the following prayer your own, and Jesus will move into your life today.

A quick warning before you make this decision. Understand that when Jesus moves in, He takes up residency. He takes His carpentry business seriously, and He doesn't give up cleaning and repairing until we become the home He knows we were created to be. With this in mind, proceed with caution:

*Lord Jesus,*

*I surrender. I give up trying to do life my own way. In the process, I have accumulated a lot of damage and hurt. I have failed to keep Your commandments, and my life (house) is in need of the Master Carpenter, to move in and take up residence.*

*Lord Jesus, forgive me for all my sins and repair my life. I desire for a smile to be back on my face, and I ask You to move in and clean house. I give my life to You and ask You to wash me in Your forgiving blood and grace.*

*Amen!*

Now, if you prayed that prayer, welcome home, all you "Teddys"!

One additional note on this: not all repairs are completed in the same amount of time. The good news is that Jesus will be with you all the days of your life, if you will follow after Him and put your trust, confidence and faith in Him and in all He accomplished at the cross for you and me.

## MY PRAYER FOR YOU

Now, allow me to conclude this portion of the book by praying for you:

*Lord Jesus,*

*I come to You today in agreement with the reader of this book. I, first and foremost, pray for the condition of our souls, that we would be right before You, covered in Your loving grace and forgiveness.*

*Father, I ask that faith would be built up in our lives, faith to believe You for anything.*

*Now, Father, I appropriate the stripes Jesus received upon His back for our healing to our own lives. I ask You right now to heal all manner of sickness and disease. Every disease bows its knee in surrender to King Jesus and, in Jesus' name, sicknesses leave our bodies now.*

*Thank You, Father!*

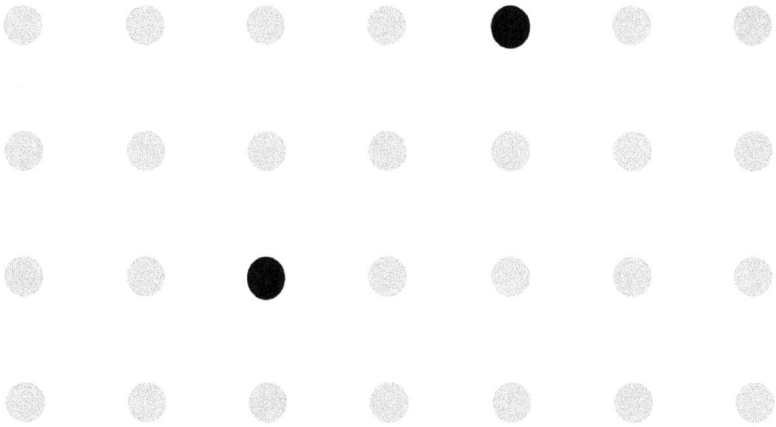

# APPENDIX A

# SCRIPTURAL DECLARATIONS

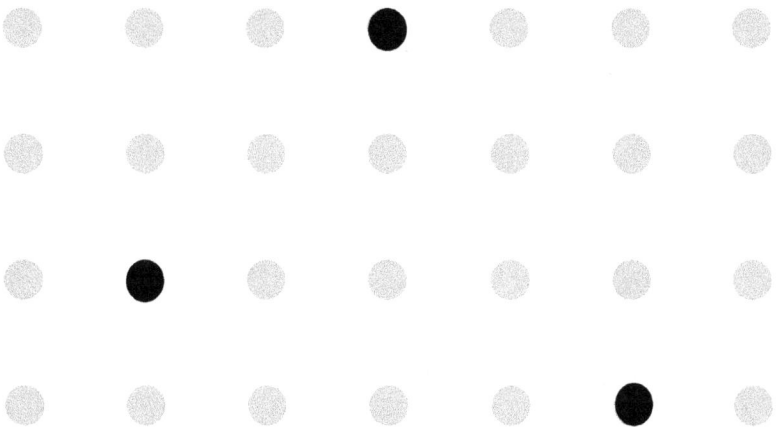

H ere are some scriptural declarations you can make that will help you focus on God's will for your life rather than on your current circumstances, whatever they may be:

## I AM...

1) A child of God (Romans 8:16)
2) Redeemed from the hand of the enemy (Psalm 107:2)
3) Forgiven (Colossians 1:13–14)
4) Saved by grace through faith (Ephesians 2:8)
5) Justified (Romans 5:1)
6) Sanctified (1 Corinthians 6:11)
7) A new creature (2 Corinthians 5:17)
8) A partaker of God's divine nature (2 Peter 1:4)
9) Redeemed from the curse of the law (Galatians 3:13)
10) Delivered from the powers of darkness (Colossians 1:13)
11) Led by the Spirit of God (Romans 8:14)
12) A son of God (Romans 8:14)
13) Kept in safety wherever I go (Psalm 91:11)
14) Getting all my needs met by Jesus (Philippians 4:19)
15) Casting all my cares on Jesus (1 Peter 5:7)
16) Strong in the Lord and in the power of His might (Ephesians 6:10)
17) Doing all things through Christ who strengthens me (Philippians 4:13)

18) An heir of God and a joint heir with Jesus (Romans 8:17)
19) Heir to the blessings of Abraham (Galatians 3:13–14)
20) Observing and doing the Lord's commandments (Deuteronomy 28:12)
21) Blessed coming in and going out (Deuteronomy 28:6)
22) An inheritor of eternal life (1 John 5:11–12)
23) Blessed with all spiritual blessings (Ephesians 1:3)
24) Healed by Jesus' stripes (1 Peter 2:24)
25) Exercising my authority over the enemy (Luke 10:19)
26) Above only and not beneath (Deuteronomy 28:13)
27) More than a conqueror (Romans 8:37)
28) Establishing God's Word here on earth (Matthew 16:19)
29) An overcomer by the blood of the Lamb and the word of my testimony (Revelation 2:11)
30) Daily overcoming the devil (1 John 4:4)
31) Not moved by what I see (2 Corinthians 4:18)
32) Walking by faith and not by sight (2 Corinthians 5:7)
33) Casting down vain imaginations (2 Corinthians 10:4–5)
34) Bringing every thought into captivity (2 Corinthians 10:5)
35) Being transformed by renewing my mind (Romans 12:1–2)
36) A laborer together with God (1 Corinthians 3:9)
37) The righteousness of God in Christ (2 Corinthians 5:21)
38) An imitator of Jesus (Ephesians 5:1)
39) The light of the world (Matthew 5:14)

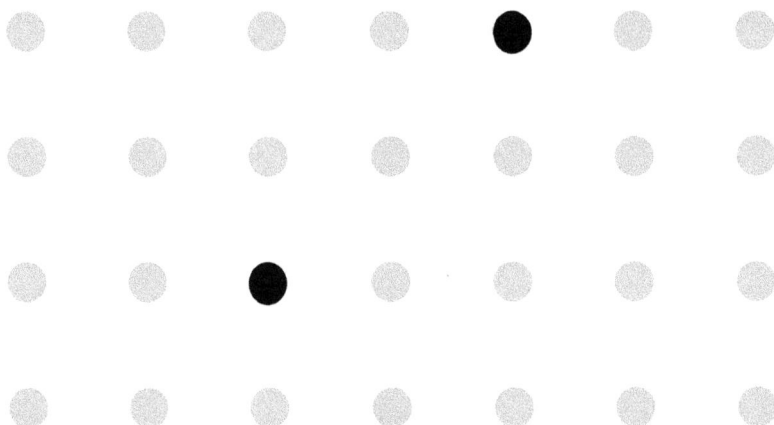

## APPENDIX B

# THE HEALING SCRIPTURES

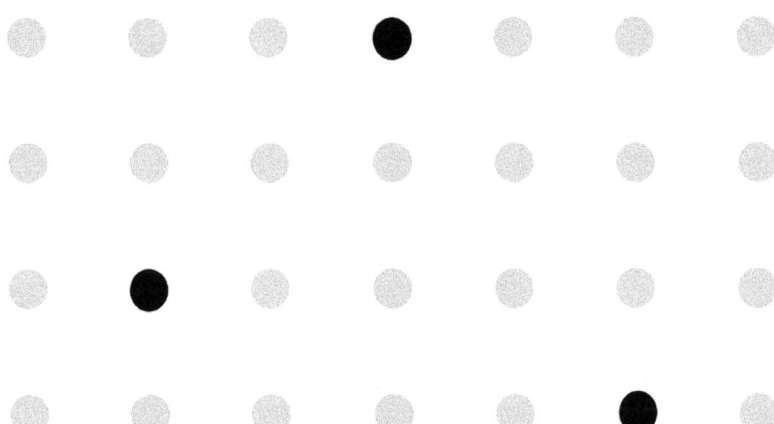

There are many passages of the sacred Scriptures that contain promises related to divine healing. Here are some that we have collected from various sources over the years, along with the variety of meanings from other versions, and some commentary and personal prayers for healing.

> **Exodus 15:25–26**—*And he cried unto the LORD; and the Lord shewed him a tree, which when he had cast into the waters, the waters were made sweet: there he made for them a statute and an ordinance, and there he proved them, and said, If thou wilt diligently hearken to the voice of the Lord thy God, and wilt do that which is right in His sight, and wilt give ear to His commandments, and keep all His statutes, I will put none of these diseases upon thee, which I have brought upon the Egyptians: for I am the Lord that healeth thee. (KJV)*

(NEB) . . . *I, the LORD, am your healer.*

(NKJV, NLT) *I am the Lord who heals you.*

(BBE) . . . *I am the LORD, your life-giver.*

(ERB) . . . *I am Yahweh, thy physician.*

(YLT) . . . *I, Jehova, am healing thee.*

(AAT) . . . *for I, the LORD, make you immune to them [diseases].*

(ESV) . . . *I am the Lord, your healer.*

God is speaking to me now, saying, "I am the Lord that healeth thee." He is watching over this Word to perform it. He is the Lord that healeth me. He is healing me now. His Word is full of healing power. I receive this Word now. I receive the healing that is in His Word now.

Healing is inherent in God's nature. God is in me. My body is a temple of God. My body is the temple of the Lord that healeth me. God is bigger than sickness and Satan. God is dwelling inside of me now, healing me now.

The Lord that healeth me is my Shepherd: I do not lack healing. My body is in contact with the Lord that healeth me. My body has to respond to God's healing life and nature at work in me now. Healing is in God and God is in me. I thank You, Father, because You are my Healer and You are healing me now. ◀

📖

**Exodus 23:25**—*And ye shall serve the* L*ORD* *your God, and He shall bless thy bread, and thy water; and I will take sickness away from the midst of thee. (KJV)*

(BBE) . . . *and give worship to the* L*ORD* *your God, who will send a blessing on your bread and on your water: and I will take all disease away from among you.*
(MNT, AAT) . . . *I will free you from disease.*
(YLT) . . . *I have turned aside sickness from thine heart.*
(ESV) . . . *I will take sickness away from among you.*
(NLT) . . . *I will protect you from illness.*

"I will" is the strongest assertion that can be made in the English language. God is speaking to me now saying, "I will take sickness away from the midst of thee." God is watching over this Word, performing it in me now. He is taking sickness away from the midst of me. I worship the Lord, my God, who takes sickness away from the midst of me. Good-bye, sickness; the Lord is taking you away from the midst of me. Thank You, Father, for taking sickness away from me. I thank You for doing what You said. ◄

📖

**Deuteronomy 7:15**—*And the Lord will take away from thee all sickness, and will put none of the evil diseases of Egypt, which thou knowest, upon thee; but will lay them upon all that hate thee. (KJV)*

(NLT) . . . *the Lord will protect you from all sickness. He will not let you suffer from the terrible diseases you knew in Egypt*

The Lord is taking away from me all sickness. His Word contains the ability to do what it says. His Word will not return void but will accomplish what it was sent to do. The Lord is taking away from me all sickness, every trace of weakness and deficiency. Sickness is going out of me now. Thank You, Father, for taking away from me all sickness, like You said. ◄

📖

**Deuteronomy 28:21–22, 27–28, 35 and 59–61**—*The LORD shall make the pestilence cleave unto thee, until he hath* *consumed thee from off the land, whither thou goest to possess it. The LORD shall smite thee with a consumption, and with a fever, and with an inflammation, and with an extreme burning, and with the sword, and with blasting, and with mildew; and they shall pursue thee until thou perish. . . . The LORD will smite thee with the botch of Egypt, and with the emerods, and with the scab, and with the itch, whereof thou canst not be healed. The LORD shall smite thee with madness, and blindness, and astonishment of heart. . . . The LORD shall smite thee in the knees, and in the legs, with a sore botch that cannot be healed, from the sole of thy foot unto the top of thy head. . . . Then the LORD will make thy plagues wonderful, and the plagues of thy seed, even great plagues, and of long continuance, and sore sicknesses, and of long continuance. Moreover he will bring upon thee all the diseases of Egypt, which thou wast afraid of; and they shall cleave unto thee. Also every sickness, and every plague, which is not written in the book of this law, them will the LORD bring upon thee until thou be destroyed. (KJV)*

## Verse 21: "Pestilence"

(GNB, BBE) *disease after disease . . .*
(NLT) *diseases*
(NKJV) *the plague*

## Verse 22: "Consumption"

(ESV, NLT) *. . . wasting disease*
(GNB) *. . . infectious diseases*
(BBE) *inflammation*

(MNT) *ague [or malarial fever]*
(TLB) *infections, extreme burning*
(AAT) *sunstroke*
(MNT) *erysipelas [a skin infection]*
(BECK, AAT) *blasting [drought]*
(TLB) *mildew [blight]*
(FENTON) *jaundice*

## Verse 27: "Botch of Egypt"
(RSV, AAT, FENTON, YLT) *ulcers*
(ERB, AAT, GNB) *sores*
(NLT, GNB, TLB, BECK, NASV, RSV, AMP) *boils, emerods*
(FENTON, TLB, MNT, NIV, AMP, NASV) *tumors*
(ERB) *hemorrhoids*
(FENTON, YLT, AAT, TLB, AMP, MNT, RSV) *scurvy*
(NASV) incurable itch
(NIV) *festering sores, itch*
(BBE) *other sorts of skin diseases*

## Verse 28: "Madness"
(GNB) *lose your mind*
(BBE) *your minds diseased, astonishment of heart*
(GNB) *confusion*
(NIV) *confusion of the mind*
(AAT) *dismay*
(AMP) *dismay of (mind and) heart*
(TLB) *fear and panic*

### Verse 35: "Sore botch"

(FENTON, YLT) *ulcers*

(ERB, AMP, GNB, BECK, NASV, NIV, TLB, RSV) *boils*

(ESV) *grievous boils*

(NBV, AAT) *sores*

(BBE) *a skin disease*

(NLT) *incurable boils*

(NKJV) *severe boils which cannot be healed*

### Verse 59: "Plagues"

(YLT) *thy strokes and the strokes of thy seed*

(NKJV) . . . *extraordinary plagues—great and prolonged plagues—and serious and prolonged sicknesses*

(GNB) . . . *incurable diseases and horrible epidemics*

(NASV) . . . *severe and lasting plagues and chronic sicknesses*

(NLT) . . . *indescribable plagues . . . intense and without relief, making you miserable and unbearably sick*

(BBE) . . . *cruel diseases stretching on through long years*

(ESV) . . . *extraordinary afflictions, . . . severe and lasting, and sicknesses grievous and lasting*

(AMP) . . . *extraordinary strokes and blows.*

### Verse 61: "Every sickness, and every plague, which is not written in the book of this law . . . until thou be destroyed"

(NIV) . . . *every kind of sickness and disaster not recorded in this Book of the Law*

(ESV) . . . *every affliction that is not recorded in the book of this law . . . until you are destroyed.*

(NLT) . . . *every sickness and plague there is, even those not mentioned in this Book of Instruction*

## Verse 65: "Trembling heart, failing of eyes, sorrow of mind"

(NIV) *an anxious mind, a despairing heart*
(NKJV) *anguish of soul*
(BBE) *a shaking heart*
(ESV) *a languishing soul*
(NLT) *your soul to despair*

Christ has redeemed me from the curse of the law. (The curse of the law is found in Deuteronomy 28. It is the curse for breaking God's law. It includes sickness, as the Scriptures above show.) Christ bought me back, brought me back, and set me free from the curse of the law. Sickness and disease are part of the curse of the law. Therefore, Christ has redeemed me from sickness. I am liberated, I am ransomed, I am free from disease. I am redeemed from every disease written in the curse of the law. (Confess your specific disease, if it is listed in these verses: "I am redeemed from _____.") I am also redeemed from every disease that is not written in the Book of the Law. Christ has redeemed me, bought me back, brought me back, and set me free from all sickness and disease. ◄

📖

**Psalm 30:2**—*O Lord my God, I cried unto thee, and thou hast healed me. (KJV)*

(NLT) . . . *you restored my health*

(NKJV) . . . *You healed me*

I believe I have received my healing (Mark 11:24). Thou hast healed me. I don't consider what I feel. I believe I am healed. Thou hast healed me. ◄

📖

**Psalm 42:11**—*Why art thou cast down, O my soul? and why art thou disquieted within me? Hope thou in God: for I shall yet praise Him, who is the health of my countenance, and my God. (KJV)*

(NKJV) . . . *the help of my countenance*

I refuse to be cast down or discouraged. I am a conqueror. I will yet praise Him Who is the health of my countenance and my God. Father, I praise You because You are the health of my countenance. ◄

📖

**Psalm 91:1–6 and 10**—*He that dwelleth in the secret place of the most High shall abide under the shadow of the Almighty. I will say of the LORD, He is my refuge and my fortress: my God; in Him will I trust. Surely He shall deliver thee from the snare of the fowler, and from the noisome pestilence. He shall cover thee with His feathers, and under His wing shalt thou trust: his truth shall be thy shield and buckler. Thou shalt not be afraid for the terror by night; nor for the arrow that* *flieth by day; nor for the pestilence that walketh in darkness; nor for the destruction that wasteth at noonday. . . . There shall no evil befall thee, neither shall any plague come nigh thy dwelling. (KJV)*

(AMP) *He who dwells in the secret place of the Most High shall remain stable and fixed under the shadow of the Almighty (Whose power no foe can withstand.)*

(ESV) *He who dwells in the shelter of the Most High will abide in the shadow of the Almighty.*

(NLT) *Those who live in the shelter of the Most High will find rest in the shadow of the Almighty.*

(RSV) *He who dwells in the shelter of the Most High, who abides in the shadow of the Almighty, will say to the* Lord, *"My refuge and my fortress; my God, in whom I trust."*

(YLT) *He who is dwelling in the secret place of the Most High, in the shade of the Mighty, lodgeth habitually, He is saying of Jehova . . . .*

(BBE) *Happy is he whose resting-place is in the secret of the* Lord, *and under the shade of the wings of the Most High; who says of the Lord, He is my safe place and my tower of strength: He is my God . . . .*

(AAT) *He who dwells . . . Says of the Lord . . . .*

(BBE) *He will take you out of the bird-net, and keep you safe from wasting disease.*

(GNB) *He will keep you safe from all hidden dangers, from all deadly disease.*

(BECK) *. . . and from the deadly plague.*

(NLT) *For he will rescue you from every trap and protect you from deadly disease.*

(TLB) *His faithful promises are your armor.*

(BBE) . . . *you will have no fear of the evil things of the night . . . or of the disease which takes men in the dark . . . .*

(BECK) . . . *the plague ravaging at noon.*

(NEB) . . . *or the plague raging at noonday.*

(NIV) . . . *nor the plague that destroys at midday.*

(BBE) *Because you have said, I am in the hands of the* LORD, *the Most High is my safe resting-place.*

(NEB) *No disaster will befall you, no calamity will come upon your home.*

(ESV) *No evil shall be allowed to befall you, no plague come near your tent.*

(AAT) *No disaster will befall you, nor calamity come near your tent.*

(GNB) . . . *and so no disaster will strike you, no violence will come near your home.*

(FENTON) *So sickness will not approach you, contagion not enter your rest.*

(NLT) *No evil will conquer you; no plague will come near your home.*

I am abiding under the shadow of the Almighty. Jehova-Rapha, the Lord that healeth me, is my refuge and fortress against disease. His Word is my shield and buckler against sickness. I am trusting under His wings, and there is healing in His wings (Malachi 4:2). I am not afraid of disease. I am not afraid of sickness. I am abiding under the shadow of Jehova-Rapha, the Lord that healeth me. No plague shall come near my dwelling or my body. I resist sickness and disease. I refuse to accept it; it is not mine. I refuse to be sick in Jesus' name. Sickness cannot trespass in my body. Sickness (name it), you can't come nigh my dwelling. I refuse you; I resist you. ◄

📖

**Psalm 103:2–3**—*Bless the* LORD, *O my soul, and forget not all His benefits: who forgiveth all thine iniquities; who healeth all thy diseases. (KJV)*

(NEB) *He pardons all my guilt and heals all my suffering.*
(BBE) *He takes away all your diseases.*
(YLT) *. . . Who is healing all thy disease.*
(NLT) *He forgives all my sins and heals all my diseases.*

Bless the Lord, Jehova-Rapha, O my soul. Blessed be God the Father. Lord, I praise You; Lord, I thank You. Praise You for Your benefits. You forgive all my sin, all my faults, all my failures and disobedience. You heal all my diseases, and I thank You for it. Healing belongs to me as part of the New Covenant. Healing is my redemptive right. (A benefit is a condition of a contract, not a bonus thrown in extra at the discretion of the employer.) Thank You, Father, for healing all my diseases. ◄

📖

**Psalm 107:20**—*He sent his word, and healed them, and delivered them from their destructions. (KJV)*

(MNT) *He sent His word to heal them and preserve their life.*
(NLT) *. . . snatching them from the door of death.*
(FENTON) *He sent out His Word, and it healed, and from their corruptions it freed!*

He sent His Word and healed me. His Word heals me and delivers me from my destructions. His Word frees me from my corruptions. God's Word contains God's ability to perform what it says (Isaiah 55:10–11). His Word is healing me now. His Word contains His healing power. His Word is working in me now. He has sent His Word and healed me. ◄

**Proverbs 4:20–22**—*My son, attend to my words; incline thine ear unto my sayings. Let them not depart from thine eyes; keep them in the midst of thine heart. For they are life unto those that find them, and health to all their flesh. (KJV)*

(TLB) . . . *let them penetrate deep within your heart.*
(NLT) . . . *for they bring life to those who find them, and healing to their whole body.*
(ERB) . . . *to every part of one's flesh they bring healing.*

God's Word is health to all my flesh. His Word is medicine to my flesh. "I am the Lord that healeth thee" is medicine to all my flesh. "I will take sickness away from the midst of thee" is medicine to my flesh. The Word of God is full of the life of God. That life is saturating my spirit. God's life and healing power is in His Word, and His Word is at work in me now. The Word of God is depositing the life of God and the healing of God into my spirit. That life and health is spreading out of my spirit into every tissue and pore of my body, creating health and soundness. My body has no choice but to respond to the healing in the Word that is being absorbed into me now. ◄

**Proverbs 12:18**—*There is that speaketh like the piercings of a sword: but the tongue of the wise is health. (KJV)*

(MNT) *A reckless tongue wounds like a sword, but there is healing power in thoughtful words.*
(GNB) *Thoughtless words can wound as deeply as any sword, but wisely spoken words can heal.*
(BBE) *There are some whose uncontrolled talk is like the wounds of a sword, but the tongue of the wise makes one well again.*
(NKJV) *. . . the tongue of the wise promotes health.*
(NLT) *. . . the words of the wise bring healing.*
(ESV) *. . . the tongue of the wise brings healing.*

My tongue makes me well. I have what I say. I say, "The Lord is my Healer." I say, "He takes sickness away from me," and "No plague can come nigh my dwelling." I say, "He healeth all my diseases." What I confess I possess. My words make me well. There is healing power in my words, for they are God's words. I speak health to every muscle, tissue, fiber, and cell in my body. I release God's healing power with my words into my whole body. Healing is mine. ◄

**Proverbs 17:22**—*A merry heart doeth good like a medicine: but a broken spirit drieth the bones. (KJV)*

(GNB) *Being cheerful keeps you healthy.*

(AAT) *A happy heart is a healing medicine.*

(BBE) *A glad heart makes a healthy body.*

(MNT) *A glad heart helps and heals.*

(ESV) *A joyful heart is good medicine.*

(NLT) *A cheerful heart is good medicine, but a broken spirit saps a person's strength.*

(FENTON) *The best medicine is a cheerful heart.*

(ERB) *A joyful heart worketh an excellent cure . . . .*

(TLB) *A broken spirit makes one sick.*

Ha, ha, ha, ha, ha, ha, ha! I have a merry heart. Sickness cannot dominate me. Satan cannot dominate me. What do you think you are trying to do, devil? You cannot put sickness on me. Ha, ha, ha, ha, ha, ha, ha, ha, I have a merry heart. I am full of joy. A merry heart works like a medicine. God's medicine is working in me. ◄

📖

**Isaiah 53:3–5**—*He is despised and rejected of men; a man of sorrows and acquainted with grief: and we hid as it were our faces from him; he was despised, and we esteemed him not. Surely he hath borne our griefs, and carried our sorrows: yet we did esteem him stricken, smitten of God, and afflicted. But he was wounded for our transgressions, he was bruised for our iniquities: the chastisement of our peace was upon him; and with his stripes we are healed. (KJV)*

(BBE) *. . . he was a man of sorrows, marked by disease*

(ERB) *. . . Man of pains and familiar with sickness.*

(NLT) . . . *acquainted with deepest grief.*

(ERB) *Yet surely our sicknesses He carried, and, as for our pains, He bare the burden of them.*

(AAT) *Yet it was our sicknesses that He bore, our pains that He carried.*

(NLT) . . . *Yet it was our weaknesses he carried.*

(ESV) . . . *with his wounds we are healed.*

(ERB) . . . *by His stripes there is healing for us.*

(NLT) . . . He was whipped so we could be healed.

(MNT) . . . *the blows that fell to Him have brought us healing.*

(GNB) . . . *we are healed by the punishment He suffered, made whole by the blows He received.*

(YLT) . . . *by His bruise there is healing to us.*

(AMP) . . . *the chastisement needful to obtain peace and well-being for us was upon Him, and with the stripes that wounded Him we are healed and made whole.*

Surely He hath borne my sickness and diseases and carried my pains. He bore them and carried them away to a distance. I don't have to bear what He bore for me. I refuse to bear what He bore for me. Satan cannot put on me what Jesus bore for me. By His stripes, I am healed. By His stripes, I got healing. By His bruises, there is healing for me. His punishment has brought me healing. Healing has been granted to me. With the stripes that wounded Him I am healed and made whole. I am made whole by the blows He received. My diseases went to the cross with Jesus and died with Him there. Satan, you are visiting the wrong one. Jesus took my sickness, and by His stripes, I am healed. ◄

📖

**Malachi 4:2**—*But unto you that fear my name shall the Sun of righteousness arise with healing in his wings; and ye shall go forth, and grow up as calves of the stall. (KJV)*

The Sun of righteousness has arisen, having conquered sickness and Satan. There is healing in His wings. That healing is beaming into me now by His Word. I am trusting beneath His healing wings. ◀

📖

**Matthew 8:2–3**—*And, behold, there came a leper and worshipped him, saying, Lord, if thou wilt, thou canst make me clean. And Jesus put forth His hand, and touched him, saying, I will; be thou clean. And immediately his leprosy was cleansed. (KJV)*

(NLT) *Suddenly, a man with leprosy approached him and knelt before him. "Lord," the man said, "if you are willing, you can heal me and make me clean." Jesus reached out and touched him. "I am willing," he said. "Be healed!" And instantly the leprosy disappeared.*
(WADE) . . . *"if You have the will, You have the power, to cleanse me." ". . . I have the will, be cleansed."*
(CPG) . . . *"Sir, if You really wanted to, You could heal me." . . . "I do want to . . . . Be healed."*
(PME) . . . *"if You want to, You can make me clean." "Of course I want to. Be clean!"*

(BBE) . . . *Lord, if it is Your pleasure, You have the power to make me clean. And He put His hand on him, saying, "It is my pleasure; be clean."*
(RIEU) . . . *"I will it. Be cleansed."*
(FENTON, WEYMOUTH, 20TH) . . . *"I am willing . . . ."*
(WUEST) . . . *I am desiring it from all my heart. Be cleansed at once.*

God wants me well. Healing is the will of God. God is at work in me right now to will and to do His good pleasure (Philippians 2:13). Healing is at work in me. ◁

📖

**Matthew 8:16–17**—*When the even was come, they brought unto him many that were possessed with devils: and He cast out the spirits with his word, and healed all that were sick: that it might be fulfilled which was spoken by Esaias the prophet, saying, Himself took our infirmities, and bare our sicknesses. (KJV)*

(NORLIE) . . . *"He took our infirmities upon Himself, and took away our diseases."*
(AMP) . . . *He Himself took (in order to carry away) our weaknesses and infirmities and bore away our diseases.*
(NEB) *"He took away our illnesses and lifted our diseases from us."*
(TRANSLATORS) . . . *"He took away our illnesses and carried away our diseases."*
(ESV) *"He took our illnesses and bore our diseases."*
(MNT) *He took away our sickness, and our diseases He removed.*

(NLV) . . . *"He took on Himself our sicknesses and carried away our diseases."*
(WUEST, NBV) . . . *carried off our diseases.*

He Himself took my infirmities and bare my sicknesses. He carried away my sicknesses. He took them away; He bore them away and removed them. Disease is not mine. Healing is mine. I refuse to bear what Jesus bore for me. I refuse to take what He took for me. Satan, you cannot put disease on me, for Jesus took my infirmities and bore my sicknesses. I refuse to accept sickness. I will not tolerate sickness. Sickness and disease is totally unacceptable. I refuse to accept it. Jesus bore them, and so I refuse to have them. ◄

**Mark 5:25–34**—*And a certain woman, which had an issue of blood twelve years, and had suffered many things of many physicians, and had spent all that she had, and was nothing bettered, but rather grew worse, when she had heard of Jesus, came in the press behind, and touched his garment. For she said, If I may touch but his clothes, I shall be whole. And straightway the fountain of her blood was dried up; and she felt in her body that she was healed of that plague. And Jesus, immediately knowing in himself that virtue had gone out of him, turned him about in the press, and said, Who touched my clothes? And his disciples said unto him, Thou seest the multitude thronging thee, and sayest thou, Who touched me? And he looked round about to see her that had done this thing. But the woman fearing and trembling, knowing what was* *done in her, came and fell down before him, and told him all the truth. And he said unto her, Daughter, thy faith hath made thee whole; go in peace, and be whole of thy plague. (KJV)*

(PEB) . . . *for she kept saying, "If I can only touch His clothes, I shall get well."*

(WUEST) . . . *for she kept saying, "If I touch even His garments, I shall me made whole."*

(PME) . . . *she kept saying . . .*

(ESV) *And Jesus, perceiving in himself that power had gone out from him . . .*

(WADE) . . . *Jesus, becoming conscious that the healing power within Him had been in active operation . . .*

(AAT) *Jesus instantly perceived that healing power had passed from Him.*

(20TH) *Jesus instantly became conscious that there had been a demand upon His powers. . . . "Your own faith has made you well. . . .*

(ESV) . . . *be healed of your disease.*

(NLT) . . . *Your suffering is over.*

(NKJV) *Be healed of your affliction.*

This woman's faith made her whole, and my faith makes me whole. I have faith, for I am a believer. I believe I receive my healing, and my faith makes me whole. The power that raised Christ from the dead is at work in me (Ephesians 1:19). My faith puts that power into active operation in my body. Disease has no choice, no chance for survival in my body. The power that raised Jesus from the dead is at work in me. That power is irresistible. It is greater than sickness and disease. That power is flowing in me and makes me whole. I am free, entirely free from sickness and disease. I am whole. I believe I have received my healing, and my faith has made me whole. ◄

📖

**Mark 16:17–18**—*And these signs shall follow them that believe; In my name shall they cast out devils; and they shall speak with new tongues; they shall take up serpents; and if they drink any deadly thing, it shall not hurt them; they shall lay hands on the sick, and they shall recover. (KJV)*

(PEB) . . . *by using my name they will drive out demons . . . .*
(MNT) . . . *for those who believe, these miracles will follow . . .*
(AAT) . . . *with my name will they drive out demons.*
(WEYMOUTH) . . . *making use of my authority, they shall expel demons.*
(TRANSLATORS) *Wherever men believe, these signs will be found.*
(WADE) *By the use of my name they will expel demons; they will speak rapturously in strange languages . . . . They will place their hands upon invalids, and they will be restored to health.*
(NLT) . . . *they will be healed.*

The name of Jesus is greater than sickness. Jesus conquered sickness and disease. In the name of Him who conquered sin, sickness and Satan, I command disease to leave my body. Satan, take your hands off my body. I cast you out in Jesus' name. You cannot do this to me. In the name of Jesus, I am free. ◄

**Luke 10:19**—*Behold, I give unto you power to tread on serpents and scorpions, and over all the power of the enemy; and nothing shall by any means hurt you. (KJV)*

(NORLIE) *I have given you authority to trample on serpents and scorpions, and over all the might of the satanic foe, and nothing will harm you in any way.*

(ESV) *. . . I have given you authority . . .*

(AMP) *Behold! I have given you authority and power to trample upon serpents and scorpions, and (physical and mental strength and ability) over all the power that the enemy [possesses], and nothing shall in any way harm you.*

(CONDON) *Yes, I have given you power to trample every evil underfoot, to counter all the might of the enemy; nothing whatever shall harm you.*

(NLT) *Look, I have given you authority over all the power of the enemy, and you can walk among snakes and scorpions and crush them. Nothing will injure you.*

Sickness is a power of the devil (Acts 10:38). I trample on all the power of the devil. I trample on disease. I stomp on disease. I tread every evil underfoot. The Lord Jesus Christ Himself gave me authority over all the power of the enemy. I have authority over sickness. Sickness, I trample on you; I tread on you; I stomp on you. Get out, get out, get out! You have no right to dominate me. Get out of my body in Jesus' name. Sickness and disease are under my feet because I am seated with Christ above all the power of the enemy (Ephesians 2:6). ◄

📖

**Luke 13:11–13 and 16**—*And, behold, there was a woman which had a spirit of infirmity eighteen years, and was bowed together, and could in no wise lift up herself. And when Jesus saw her, he called her to him, and said unto her, Woman, thou art loosed from thine infirmity. And he laid his hands on her; and immediately she was made straight, and glorified God.... And ought not this woman, being a daughter of Abraham, whom Satan hath bound, lo, these eighteen years, be loosed from this bond on the Sabbath day? (KJV)*

(AMP) . . . *an infirmity caused by a spirit [a demon of sickness].*
(PEB) . . . *had a disease caused by an evil spirit; she was bent double and altogether unable to hold herself up.*
(NASB) . . . *a sickness caused by a spirit.*
(WUEST) . . . *A woman had a spirit that caused an infirmity eighteen years and was completely bent together by a curvature of the spine, and was not able to raise herself up at all.*
(NLT) . . . *a woman who had been crippled by an evil spirit . . . bent double for eighteen years and was unable to stand up straight . . .*
(NASB) . . . *you are freed from your sickness.*
(BBE) . . . *you are made free from your disease.*
(NIV) . . . *you are set free from your infirmity.*
(NORLIE) . . . *you are now rid of your infirmity.*
(PEB) . . . *you are freed from your disease.*
(NLT) . . . *you are healed of your sickness.*

(CPG)... *"Lady, you have been freed from your weakness."*

(WORRELL)... *"Woman, you have been loosed from your infirmity."*

(CONDON)... *"Your bondage is at an end."*

(PEB) . . . *at once she straightened herself up and burst into praising God.*

(ERB)... *was there not a needs-be that she be loosed . . . ?*

(WADE) *And ought not this woman, a descendant of Abraham as she is, whose power of movement Satan has fettered actually for seventeen years, to have been released from such fetters on the day of the Sabbath?*

(NLT) *Isn't it right that she be released, even on the Sabbath?*

(BBE) *And is it not right for this daughter of Abraham, who has been in the power of Satan for eighteen years, to be made free on the Sabbath?*

(NORLIE) *But this woman, a daughter of Abraham, who has been in the bondage of Satan—think of it!—for eighteen years, should not have the right to be released from her bonds because it is the Sabbath?*

Satan cannot bind me with sickness. I have been delivered from Satan's dominion and translated into the kingdom of the Son of God (Colossians 1:13). Sickness is ungodly. Sickness is of the devil. Satan, you cannot put sickness on me. Who do you think you are? You are a defeated foe. Jesus stripped you of your authority over me (Colossians 2:15 and Hebrews 2:14). You cannot do this to me. I resist you in Jesus' name. I am delivered. I am free; I have been loosed. I am no longer fettered. I am now rid of my infirmity. My bondage is at an end! It is right for me to be completely free, for I am a child of Abraham, and Abraham's blessings are mine (Galatians 3:14 and 29). Healing is part of the covenant, and I am under the covenant. Therefore healing is mine. Healing belongs to me. It is my rightful possession. I have a right to be released. Satan, I demand my rights now. Take your filthy hands off of my body! ◄

📖

**John 14:12–14**—*Verily, verily, I say unto you, He that believeth on me, the works that I do shall he do also; and greater works than these shall he do; because I go unto my Father. And whatsoever ye shall ask in my name, that will I do, that the Father may be glorified in the Son. If ye shall ask anything in my name, I will do it. (KJV)*

The name of Jesus takes the place of Jesus. Jesus is the resurrected healing Lord. In the name of Jesus I command disease to leave my body. My body is healed in Jesus' name. His name through faith in His name gives me perfect soundness (Acts 3:16). I am healed in Jesus' name. ◄

📖

**John 15:4–5**—*Abide in me, and I in you. As the branch cannot bear fruit of itself, except it abide in the vine; no more can ye, except ye abide in me. I am the vine, ye are the branches: he that abideth in me, and I in him, the same bringeth forth much fruit: for without me ye can do nothing. (KJV)*

(NLV) *Get your life from Me and I will live in you. No branch can give fruit by itself. It has to get life from the vine. You are able to give fruit only when you have life from Me. I am the Vine and you are the branches. Get your life from me. Then I will live in you and you will give much fruit. You can do nothing without Me.*

*(PME) You must go on growing in me and I will grow in you. For just as the branch cannot bear any fruit unless it shares the life of the vine, so you can produce nothing unless you go on growing in me. I am the vine itself; you are the branches. It is the man who shares my life and whose life I share who proves fruitful. For the plain fact is that apart from me you can do nothing at all.*

I am in union with Christ. My spirit is in union with Christ the Healer. I draw out His healing power, and it is manifested in my body. I am one with the healing Vine. I am in union with the healing Christ. I have His life and health in me. ◄

**Acts 3:16**—*And his name through faith in his name hath made this man strong, whom ye see and know; yea, the faith which is by him hath given him this perfect soundness in the presence of you all. (KJV)*

His name, through faith in His name, makes me whole, gives me perfect soundness, and makes me strong. The name of Jesus is greater than sickness. All that He is in His name. All that He did is in His name. He is greater than sickness. He conquered sickness. I speak His name, Jesus, to my body now. Every disease germ dies now in Jesus' name. My body is made whole in Jesus' name. ◄

**Acts 10:38**—*How God anointed Jesus of Nazareth with the Holy Ghost and with power: who went about doing good, and healing all that were oppressed of the devil; for God was with him.*

(MNT) . . . *all who were harassed by the devil . . .*
(NIV, PEB) . . . *healing all who were under the power of the devil.*
(RIEU) . . . *healing everyone in the devil's clutches . . .*
(BV) . . . *curing all those who were under the tyranny of the devil.*
(NBV) . . . *healing all that were overpowered by the devil . . .*
(WEYMOUTH) . . . *curing all who were crushed by the power of the devil.*
(CPG) . . . *God equipped Him with the Holy Spirit and power, Who passed through our midst acting nobly and healing all those who were lorded over by the devil . . . .*
(PME) . . . *healing all who suffered from the devil's power . . .*
(NLT) . . . *healing all who were troubled by the devil*
(AMP) . . . *harassed and oppressed by [the power of] the devil . . .*

Sickness is an oppression of the devil. Satan cannot oppress me with sickness, for I have been delivered from his authority (Colossians 1:13). Satan cannot oppress me. I have authority to tread on Satan and demons and all the power the enemy possesses. I tread on sickness. Satan, you cannot lord it over me with foul disease. You cannot do this to me. Sickness, you cannot do this to me. You are visiting the wrong one. Healing is mine. The power that raised Jesus from the dead is at work in me. It is healing power because He is the Lord that healeth. Healing power is at work in me, and I AM FREE! ◄

📖

**Romans 8:2**—*For the law of the Spirit of life in Christ Jesus hath made me free from the law of sin and death. (KJV)*

(TRANSLATORS) *For the principle of spiritual life in Christ Jesus has liberated me from the principle of sin and death.*
(AMP) . . . *[the law of our new being]* . . .

📖

**Romans 8:11**—*But if the Spirit of him that raised up Jesus from the dead dwell in you, he that raised up Christ from the dead shall also quicken your mortal bodies by his Spirit that dwelleth in you. (KJV)*

(WAY) *If the Spirit of God, of Him who raised Jesus from the dead, has its home in you, then He who raised the Messiah Jesus from the dead will thrill with a new life your very bodies—those mortal bodies of yours—by the agency of His own Spirit, which now has its home in you.*
(AAT) *If the Spirit of Him who raised Jesus from the dead has taken possession of you, He who raised Christ Jesus from the dead will also give your mortal bodies life through His Spirit that has now taken possession of you.*
(GODBEY) . . . *will also create life in your mortal bodies* . . .

The Spirit of God is residing in me. The Spirit of God is making His home in my spirit. The Spirit of Jehova-Rapha is in me, giving life to my body. The Spirit of the Lord that healeth is creating life, supplying life in my body, making it whole. The life of Jehova-Rapha is being applied to my body by His Spirit who dwells in me. The life of God drives out every trace of sickness and disease. The life of God is destroying disease germs in my body now. ◄

📖

**1 Corinthians 6:13, 15 and 19–20**—*Meats for the belly, and the belly for meats: but God shall destroy both it and them. Now the body is not for fornication, but for the Lord; and the Lord for the body. . . . Know ye not that your bodies are the members of Christ? Shall I then take the members of Christ, and make them the members of an harlot? God forbid. . . . What? Know ye not that your body is the temple of the Holy Ghost which is in you, which ye have of God, and ye are not your own? For ye are bought with a price: therefore glorify God in your body, and in your spirit, which are God's. (KJV)*

My body wasn't made for sin but for the Lord. My body wasn't made for sickness, but for the Lord. My body is a member of Christ. My body belongs to Christ. Satan cannot make Christ's body sick. Satan, how dare you trespass on God's property? Take your hands off God's property in Jesus' name. My body is the temple of Jehova-Rapha, the Lord that healeth. He is in me, healing me now, for He is the Lord that healeth me. I have been bought with a price. Jesus' blood cleanses me from all sin, and by His stripes, my body is healed. I glorify God in my body. I refuse to allow disease in my body in Jesus' name. You foul disease, take your hands off my body in Jesus' name. ◄

📖

**Galatians 2:20**—*I am crucified with Christ: nevertheless I live; yet not I, but Christ liveth in me; and the life which I now live in the flesh I live by the faith of the Son of God, who loved me, and gave himself for me. (KJV)*

(LAUBACH) . . . *Christ took me to the cross with Him, and I died there with Him.*
(ASV, NASV, RSV, NEB and NIV) *I have been crucified with Christ. . . .*

I was crucified with Christ. I died with Him to sickness and disease. Christ the Healer lives in me. Healing is in me. Christ in me heals me. ◄

📖

**Galatians 3:13**—*Christ hath redeemed us from the curse of the law, being made a curse from us; for it is written, Cursed is everyone that hangeth on a tree. (KJV)*

(TRANSLATORS) *Christ ransomed us from the curse of the law, by taking that curse upon Himself for our sakes . . . .*
(WAND) *Now, Christ bought us off the curse of the law at the cost of being accursed for our sakes . . . .*

(20TH) *Christ ransomed us from the curse pronounced in the law....*
(WEYMOUTH) *Christ has purchased our freedom....*

**Philippians 2:13**—*For it is God which worketh in you both to will and to do of His good pleasure. (KJV)*

God is at work in me. Jehovah-Rapha is at work in me, healing me. He is the Lord that healeth me. God is greater than the devil. Healing is greater than sickness. God is at work in me, healing me. ◄

📖

**Ephesians 4:27**—*Neither give place to the devil. (KJV)*

(PEB) *Stop giving the devil a chance.*
(BV) *Give the devil no place or opportunity in your life.*
(TRANSLATORS) *... and do not give the devil a chance.*
(CPG) *... don't give in one inch to the devil.*

I refuse to give place to the devil. Sickness and disease are of the devil. Satan, you cannot put that on my body. You cannot, you cannot, you cannot. I say "no," and I mean "no." No sickness or plague comes nigh my dwelling. You have the wrong address. I will not give in once inch. Satan, you have no place in my body. I belong to God. Sickness, you have no choice but to go, because I am not giving you a chance. Get out now. ◄

**Colossians 1:12**—*Giving thanks unto the Father, which hath made us meet to be partakers of the inheritance of the saints in light. (KJV)*

(AAT) *... thank the Father who has entitled you to share the lot of God's people in the realm of light.*
(NBV) *... Who has qualified you for your share in the inheritance of the saints in the light.*
(ERB) *... the Father that hath made you sufficient for your share ...*
(GODBEY) *... Who has made us worthy ...*
(NORLIE) *... He enabled us to share the inheritance of the saints who live in the light.*
(TLB) *... to share all the wonderful things that belong to those who live in the kingdom of light.*

I am qualified, entitled, worthy, and able to partake of my inheritance in Christ. Healing belongs to me (Psalms 102:3). I refuse to be beaten out of my inheritance. ◄

**Colossians 1:13**—Who hath delivered us from the power of darkness, and hath translated us into the kingdom of his dear Son. (KJV)
(AAT) *He has rescued us from the dominion of darkness, and has transferred us into the realm of the His dear Son.*
(PEB) *He has freed us from the power of darkness and carried us away into the kingdom of His beloved Son.*

(CONEYBEARE) *For He has delivered us from the dominion of darkness, and translated us into the kingdom of His beloved Son.*
(WADE) *For God has rescued us from the dominance exercised by the powers of spiritual darkness, and transferred us to the dominion of His Son—the object of His love.*
(TLB) *For He has rescued us out of the darkness and gloom of Satan's kingdom and brought us into the kingdom of His dear Son.*

I have been delivered from the authority of darkness. I have been delivered from Satan's authority and dominion (Acts 26:18). I am free from Satan's dominion. Sickness is of the devil. Satan cannot dominate me with sickness a d disease. Satan, I have been delivered from your authority. You cannot put sickness on me. I have passed out of your jurisdiction over into the Kingdom of the Son of God. I am a citizen in the Kingdom of Jehova-Rapha, the Lord that healeth me. I have been transplanted into the Kingdom of His Son. ◄

📖

**Colossians 1:14**—*In whom we have redemption through his blood, even the forgiveness of sins. (KJV)*

(AAT) ... *by whom we have been ransomed from captivity* ...
(CONEYBEARE) ... *in whom we have our redemption* ...
(WAY) ... in whom we have our ransoming, the remission of our sins.

In Christ Jesus, I have redemption. I have been ransomed from captivity. I am delivered from Satan and his works. I am free from sickness and disease. ◄

📖

**James 4:7**—*Submit yourselves therefore to God. Resist the devil, and he will flee from you. (KJV)*

(NEB) *Stand up to the devil and he will turn and run.*
(WUEST) *Stand immovable against the onset of the devil, and he will flee from you.*
(BBE) *. . . be ruled by God; but make war on the Evil One, and he will be put to flight before you.*

I submit to God. I submit to the will of God. I accept the authority of God and His Word. I submit to God's Word. I resist you, devil. I resist disease. You cannot do this to my body. Get out. Remove yourself. You must flee from my body now. ◄

📖

**James 5:15–16**—*And the prayer of faith shall save the sick, and the Lord shall raise him up; and if he hath committed sins, they shall be forgiven him. Confess your faults one to another and pray one for another, that ye may be healed. The effectual fervent prayer of a righteous man availeth much. (KJV)*

(BBE) *And by the prayer of faith the man who is ill will be made well.*
(WADE) *. . . and the prayer offered in faith will restore the sufferer to health, and the Lord will raise him from his sickbed.*

The prayer of faith has made me whole. The Lord is raising me up. I cannot stay down. I believe I received when I prayed, and my faith makes me whole. I believe I have received my healing. ◄

📖

**1 Peter 2:24**—*Who his own self bare our sins in his own body on the tree, that we, being dead to sins, should live unto righteousness: by whose stripes ye were healed. (KJV)*

(20TH*) . . . His bruising was your healing.*
(ESV) *By his wounds you have been healed.*

By His stripes I was healed. Healing belongs to me. I was healed 2000 years ago by the stripes Jesus bore. By His stripes I was healed. I am not trying to get healing. I have healing because by His stripes I was healed. ◄

📖

**1 Peter 5:8–9**—*Be sober, be vigilant; because your adversary the devil, as a roaring lion, walketh about, seeking whom he may devour: whom resist steadfast in the faith, knowing that the same afflictions are accomplished in your brethren that are in the world. (KJV)*

(NLT) Stand firm against him, and be strong in your faith.
(WUEST) *Stand immovable against his onset, solid as a rock in your faith . . .*

(AMP) . . . *be firm in faith (against his onset)rooted, established, strong, immovable and determined . . . .*

I stand immovable against sickness in Jesus' name. I refuse to accept it. ◄

📖

**1 John 3:8**—*He that committeth sin is of the devil, for the devil sinneth from the beginning. For this purpose the Son of God was manifested, that he might destroy the works of the devil. (KJV)*

(AMP) *The reason the Son of God was made manifest (visible) was to undo (destroy, loosen and dissolve) the works the devil (has done).*
(YLT) *. . . that He might break up the works of the devil.*
(BBE) *. . . and the Son of God was seen on earth so that He might put an end to the works of the evil one.*
(WAND) *. . . that He might neutralize what the devil has done.*
(WUEST) *. . . that He might bring to naught the works of the devil.*
(CPG) *. . . that He might break up the devil's doings.*
(ESV) *The reason the Son of God appeared was to destroy the works of the devil.*
(PME) *Now the son of God came to the earth with the express purpose of liquidating the devil's activities.*

Sickness is a work of the devil. Jesus came to destroy the works of the devil. Sickness has been dissolved, broken up, annulled, undone, liquidated, as far as I am concerned. Jesus put sickness to an end for me. The activities of the devil have been liquidated. ◄

**3 John 2**—*Beloved, I wish above all things that thou mayest prosper and be in health, even as they soul prospereth. (KJV)*

I am prospering, and I am in health, even as my soul prospers, because it is God's will for me. God is at work in me to do His will and pleasure. Jehovah-Rapha is at work in me, healing me. ◄

# YOU MAY CONTACT THE AUTHOR IN ANY OF THE FOLLOWING WAYS:

**Mail:**
MercyGate Church
Pastor Don Gibson Ministries
P.O. Box 40
Mont Belvieu, Texas 77580

**Donald Gibson Ministries:**
Don@donaldgibsonministries.com

**Telephone:**
(281) 576-5201

**eMail:**
dgibson@mercygatechurch.com

**Internet:**
www.mercygatechurch.com